Pre-empt Prevent Protect Pre-empt Prevent Protect Pre-empt Prevent Protect Pre-empt Prevent Protect Pre-empt Prevent Protect Pre-empt Prevent Protect Pre-empt Prevent Protect Pre-empt Prevent Protect Pre-empt Prevent Protect Pre-empt Prevent Protect Pre-empt Prevent Protect Pre-empt Prevent Protect Pre-empt Prevent Protect Pre-empt

PRE-EMPT
PREVENT
PROTECT

Chris Holt is a personal security consultant with extensive experience in counterterrorism, personal protection, advanced driving techniques, first aid and self-defence. He has had to look after himself and others in the most dangerous places in the world.

Before leaving the British Army, Chris spent most of his career as a bomb disposal officer. Before he was 30, he commanded counterterrorist and bomb disposal operations in Iraq, the Balkans and the UK mainland. He was also an Army Diver and Commando and was appointed MBE in 2005 for services to Bomb Disposal.

PRE-EMPT
PREVENT
PROTECT

PERSONAL
SECURITY
HANDBOOK

CHRIS HOLT

SUTTON PUBLISHING

Sutton Publishing Limited
Phoenix Mill · Thrupp · Stroud
Gloucestershire · GL5 2BU

First published 2007

Copyright © Chris Holt, 2007

Chris Holt has asserted the moral right to be
identified as the author of this work.

British Library Cataloguing in Publication Data
A catalogue record for this book is available
from the British Library.

ISBN 978-0-7509-4562-2 (HB)
ISBN 978-0-7509-4563-9 (PB)

Designed by Glad Stockdale
Illustrated by John Lawson
Commissioned photography by Lynwen Griffiths

Typeset in RotisSansSerif
Typesetting and origination by
Sutton Publishing Limited.
Printed and bound in England by
J.H. Haynes & Co. Ltd, Sparkford.

While every effort has been made to ensure that the
information given in this book is accurate, the
publishers and the author do not accept responsibility
for any errors or omissions or for any changes in the
details given in this handbook or for the consequences
of any reliance on the information provided.

Contents

Acknowledgements

In producing this book many people have been involved on a professional and voluntary basis. The Red Cross has been hugely helpful, as have a number of friends in various UK agencies. Thank you to you all for your comments and advice. You know who you are. John Lawson put up with more than a little interference to produce the illustrations and Lynwen Griffiths has done a wonderful job with her camera. Andy, Becki and Dicky were fantastic volunteer models who agreed to do some unusual things and be photographed – thank you. The team at Suttons have been remarkable in their patience and instruction and although there were a huge amount of people involved I should personally thank Jeremy, Jonathan, Jim, Yvette, Julia and Glad. Most importantly there are two people who probably deserve to have their names on the front cover. Hilary Walford has worked tirelessly to bring the book together and has acted far beyond her brief. I hope it was all worth it in the end. Finally of course I must thank my wife, Caroline, who, apart from spending hours checking copy and searching for images, kept me going throughout the process of pulling it all together. She is an inspiration, and I look forward to her first book.

Introduction

L ife in the twenty-first century is easier for most of us than it was for our ancestors. While statistically speaking we have never lived so long or been so safe, life today holds its own particular dangers. In a world where distance does little to halt the spread of information, most of us are acutely aware of acts of violence happening all over the world.

You will find no information in this book on how to garrotte an Afghan terrorist with your dental floss or how to survive in the wilderness by licking the morning dew from leaves. What you will find is detail on the security issues most likely to affect you during your life, whether crime or terrorism, at home or abroad. This book will give you the advice you need, and the confidence to do something proactive about your own security.

Whether you are a city worker wanting to understand more about a terrorist attack, a student living away from home for the first time or a member of a hen or stag party travelling to Central Europe, this book has something for you. Read it and keep it with you as a reference, safe in the knowledge that, by doing something rather than nothing, you are already making a difference to your own safety.

HOW TO USE THIS BOOK

It is possible to pick this book up and read it from cover to cover. However, many of you will want to delve in and out of the book or refer back to advice once you have reached the last page. In order to make it easier to do this, the content has been deliberately broken down into bite-sized chunks that you can digest piecemeal. In some cases this means that advice on general principles has been repeated. Interspersed throughout the book are detailed illustrations highlighting some of the key issues discussed.

While this book brings together a wide range of information on crime and terrorism, the only person who can make a decision on what to do with that material is you. The overall aim is to allow you to make more informed threat assessments in your everyday life.

I can tell you my thoughts on particular subjects and I hope you find them useful. They draw not only on my own experience but also on that of friends and colleagues in almost every area of UK counterterrorism and law enforcement. It is you who has to consider that information and then make a decision on how to use it.

LANGUAGE

As with any specialist subject matter, it is worth examining at the outset some of the general language used. You will find the terms 'threat' and 'risk' used throughout this book, and definitions from *The New Oxford Dictionary of English* are as follows:

Threat

1. *a statement of an intention to inflict pain, injury, damage, or other hostile action on someone in retribution for something done or not done;*
2. *a person or thing likely to cause damage or danger.*

Risk

1.   *a situation involving exposure to danger;*
2.   *the possibility that something unpleasant or*
       unwelcome will happen.

It is possible to use the term 'threat' in a number of contexts. You will often hear a person or organisation identified as 'posing a threat'. It is also often for the media or politicians to refer to a 'threat state'. This reflects the likelihood of some form of attack, normally as predicted by the security services.

With regards to risk, it is possible to say of almost anything that it 'may happen'. This is a meaningless statement, and it has been avoided in the book. To identify the 'risk' you are *actually* exposed to, meaningful statistics have been included where relevant and possible in an attempt to place threats into context. In this way I hope to temper some of the hype that surrounds terrorist activity in particular, and to give you a better feel about the likelihood of you personally becoming involved.

If a threat exists – for example, from a terrorist bomb or from a mugger who needs to fuel a drug dependency – you probably cannot personally reduce it. But you *can* reduce the risk you are exposed to. This forms the basis of the approach in this book: PRE-EMPT, PREVENT, PROTECT.

THREAT ASSESSMENT

In many cases in this book, you will be given background information and advice but told that any decision to act should be based on your own threat assessment. This is the basic tool of PRE-EMPT, PREVENT, PROTECT. In almost all instances, this is not some complex activity that requires a pen and paper, but a rapid and conscious mental process that results in a decision and an action.

Threat assessment is something many of you will already practise in your work life, although you may call it something else. Certainly, you already conduct assessments instinctively when you are confronted with a threat to your personal security. For example, I hope that most of you would decide not to enter a bank if you saw a masked man with a gun through the window!

When making a threat assessment you will instinctively consider the threat triad of location, type and aim:

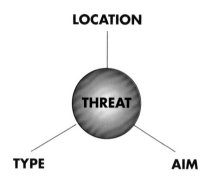

LOCATION

THREAT

TYPE   **AIM**

In any situation, if you believe you are at risk, then you need to act. For example, if you see an individual with a knife in his hand and he is in your path and you believe he is going to try to rob you, you need to act. If one of the three elements of location, type or aim is missing, you may act differently, or you may not need to act at all:

○ *Location of threat. If the same individual is armed and you still believe he wants to rob you, but he is on the opposite side of a railway line and separated from you by a double fence, he is probably no longer a threat to you, but you should still monitor him until you have passed him.*

○ *Type of threat. If the same individual is in front of you and you believe he wants to rob you, but he no longer has a knife, he is a significantly lower threat. You*

*should still try to avoid the location, but you should
reconsider the amount of force you might be prepared
to use to defend yourself.*

Aim of the threatening person. *If you look again and
see that the individual in your path is carrying a knife,
but is actually a butcher whom you recognise, outside
his shop, and that his aim is to cut down a display
poster, you can continue without action.*

In all instances you can make a threat assessment only if you have
observed the environment around you, and identified threats
before you are involved with them. In Chapter 1 you will learn
about situational awareness and how to take back responsibility
for your own security.

PRE-EMPT, PREVENT, PROTECT

Identifying ways to create and then maintain your personal
security is the theme of this book, and I have loosely summarised
this approach as the 'three Ps' of PRE-EMPT, PREVENT, PROTECT.
Whatever situation or location you find yourself in, you can
guarantee you are better off if you identify the threats around you
and determine the risk you are exposed to by conducting a quick
threat assessment (PRE-EMPT). Armed with this information, you
should take positive action to avoid your involvement with any
threat you have identified (PREVENT). And to ensure permanent
reassurance and personal confidence, you should maintain a
constant level of physical protection for yourself and your
belongings and be mentally and physically equipped to defend
yourself if required (PROTECT). Your actions should not have to
alter drastically from place to place; all that should change are the
location and type of threat you are exposed to. Moreover, you
should not be required to change your way of life or daily habits.

MORE HELP

This book brings together a wide variety of open source information and draws upon the experience of the author and other security professionals to place that sometimes complex information into context. If you need more help, there are experts whose job it is to offer you qualified and up-to-date advice. Whether you are an individual worried about home security and need to talk to the police, or a general manager concerned about your business continuity plans and interested in the advice of MI5, the list of Websites and Sources of Further Information at the back of this book will act as a useful start point. There is no such thing as a stupid question when it comes to your own security, so take a personal interest and take control.

REALISTIC ASSESSMENT

While you are reading this book, you will become aware of many simple ways to keep yourself safe in everyday life. Statistics are included to make you feel more confident about the real risks you are exposed to. You may well feel that some of the content is slightly paranoid in identifying everything that could possibly go wrong. This is a valid observation, and there is no doubt that it would be a tremendously unlucky person who actually experienced a fraction of the crimes or incidents discussed. However, if, by reading the whole book, you become more aware of your actions and have some idea of how to react during the one time in your life when your personal security is threatened, then it will be worthwhile. Please enjoy the book, consider it and discuss it. Most of all, remember that the chances of being involved in a terrorist incident or a violent crime are very, very small, and that by making a little bit of effort you can make a massive amount of difference to your personal security. So take control and stop worrying; **stay safe and start living**.

Situational Awareness

I n this first chapter we will discuss the kinds of behaviour and attitude that you should consider no matter what environment you find yourself in. Most people living in a modern Western country are almost completely unaware of the risks they expose themselves to on a routine basis. There is a genuine and frankly probable threat of physical injury from 'low-level' street crime or from a car crash, yet somehow this has not manifested itself in a change in our activity or an increase in our general awareness. We just seem to accept that in the modern world we might be mugged on the street or involved in a driving incident. Conversely, many city dwellers are acutely aware of the risks of terrorism, which in statistical terms is far less likely to affect our lives.

It is a sad fact that many people experience fear and change their behaviour because of a false perception of reality. Increasing your situational awareness can free you from the anxieties that you may have developed from listening too closely to the media. It also allows you to make informed decisions about which actions are safe and which are not worth the risk. You will find guidance in this chapter on how not to look like a victim, including advice on how to present yourself, how to carry your belongings and how to improve your observation skills.

This advice applies just as much to how you should conduct yourself in London as it does to what you should be thinking about if you are travelling in central Africa. It has such a wide application because it is based on human nature and how people interact the world over. None of the advice should lead you to have to change the way you lead your life; that would be pointless. It should complement your current routine and allow you to feel more confident.

ARE YOU A VICTIM?

The two pictures below show the same man. In each image he is carrying £50 in cash, a mobile phone, a laptop, an MP3 player and a digital camera. Step into the mind of a criminal and decide which image represents someone you are going to rob. It's an easy choice, but why?

Consider the following criteria and think in each case how you normally appear to the potential criminal.

The way you hold yourself and carry your belongings, and how aware you are of your surroundings, can reduce the chance of a criminal seeing you as a victim.

PRE-EMPT

Posture. In the left-hand image our model is standing tall. His body posture suggests that he is fit and alert (funny how you can always spot an off-duty soldier). This is normally an indication of confidence, and along with that goes the likelihood that this person will react if confronted. In the right-hand image he is in a relaxed posture and does not appear to be ready to react. While it is unlikely that you will change your bearing overnight, it is worth considering that the way you hold yourself if you feel threatened may affect the decision a criminal makes. Stand tall and don't look like a victim.

Eye contact. The criminal is to a certain extent a hunter; he would much rather attack an unsuspecting prey. By maintaining situational awareness, our alert model has identified the observer as a potential criminal and has gained eye contact (funny how you can always spot an off-duty police officer). Eye contact in itself can be disarming, but be very cautious about sustaining it, as this can lead to aggression in individuals with already heightened emotions and also in certain cultural groups.

Ability to defend. If you have ever had the opportunity to watch a professional close protection team or bodyguard, you will notice that they will refuse point blank to carry anything for the person they are protecting. Their job is to react, and it is difficult to do that with your hands full. While sometimes it is inevitable that you have to carry something in your hands, there is almost always a better way of securing your belongings about your body. Your clothing and footwear are also worth considering. 'Always wear shoes you can run down a set of stairs in' is a good bench-mark for many reasons!

Use eye contact to your advantage.

Carrying belongings. We will cover this in more detail below, but note that our good example is not advertising his belongings to a potential criminal and has them secured about his person.

Intent/attitude. This is the most difficult concept to define or explain, but is the most important. In the pictures we asked our model first to project the message 'you are not having my bag' and then to think 'just leave me alone'. This again comes down to confidence and your ability to project yourself as someone who is not prepared to be a victim. Do not be fooled into thinking this has anything to do with size or build; intent can make anyone scary. Remember, the criminal will always take the easy option; it's what being a criminal is all about. In most situations, by not appearing to be the easiest victim, you will dissuade any kind of attacker.

CARRYING AND SECURING YOUR BELONGINGS

Day kit

Most of us will always carry a few essential items, which we will call 'day kit'. Apart from a wallet or purse, your day kit will normally include, but is not limited to, loose change, a set of keys, a

We all carry valuable items routinely as our day kit.

PRE-EMPT

phone, a pair of sunglasses and increasingly a camera and MP3 player. Hopefully I can encourage you to add a panic alarm to this list. On a winter's day we will all wear some kind of large jacket, which is likely to have internal zipped pockets that are ideal for securing belongings. So here we will consider our summer clothing and how we carry our belongings in warmer weather.

For women the 'pocket on a bit of string' or handbag is probably the only place you will consider keeping your day kit. This actually makes sound security sense, but if you have all your eggs in one basket, make sure you look after the basket. A handbag for normal daily use should always have a securing mechanism so that you can keep it closed while it is on your shoulder. Best of all is a bag with a flap and a zip.

Try to keep your bag within your peripheral vision.

The flap-and-zip closure ensures that, should someone try to delve into your bag – for example, on a crowded tube train – your belongings are out of reach. When you are out in a restaurant or bar, always keep your bag with you. The bag hanger is a great

You can use a number of strategies to keep your handbag close to you.

device. It allows you to hang your bag next to you wherever you are; I am told it can even solve the 'what to do when I'm dancing' problem, as a spot to hang your bag can normally be found around the side of a dance floor. Cloakrooms in nightclubs and restaurants are not places to leave anything of value except a coat.

For men there are a number of options for carrying your day kit. The popularity of the 'man bag' is cyclical, but if you do choose to carry a male handbag, the same advice applies as it does for women; keep it near you and

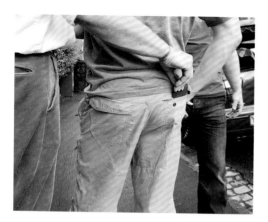

ensure it closes securely. On a sunny afternoon, men will probably cram their day kit into their trouser pockets, with perhaps a phone in a top pocket and their sunglasses on the top of their heads. This is not something that you're likely to change, but it is worth considering what goes where.

Pickpockets working in teams know where most people carry their valuables.

Most of us carry things in the same place, depending on whether we are left- or right-handed. Right-handed men tend to carry loose change in their front right pocket (normally balanced with keys in the front left) and their wallet in their rear right pocket. What can we learn from this? A criminal who is attempting to pickpocket you is likely to decide whether you are right- or left-handed and target the rear pocket on that side. An easy solution is to move your wallet to your front pocket whenever you are in a busy place – for example, a train or bar. Better still, change your habit permanently and try to keep anything of value in your front pockets, where you can feel it. Another tactic used by the pickpocket is to get an accomplice to rub against you. If we feel something suspicious, we tend to check that our wallet is still there. From your check, he can see where you are keeping your belongings and better target those areas. If you are bumped, try to resist the immediate desire to check your wallet; have a look around first and then check.

Consider what actually needs to be in your wallet or purse when you go out.

PRE-EMPT

The easiest way to minimise the effect of any robbery is to reduce the amount of kit you carry. When you leave the house, consider whether you really need your driving licence, all your credit cards or your gym membership card. If you're heading off to an area you know is high risk – for example, a night out in town – it's a good idea to buy a small wallet or purse specifically for that purpose. It can contain cash, a travel card and perhaps a credit card. Leave everything else at home. That way, if you do get robbed, the impact is minimal.

Do you really always need your full set of keys or just a front door key? By having a simple karabiner-style snap lock, you can separate out your keys and take with you only what you need. Reducing what you take with you each time you leave the house will minimise the impact of any loss.

A small clip on your keys allows you to leave the majority of them at home when you go out.

Mobile phones and MP3 players

A significant majority of street crimes involve the robbery of mobile phones and MP3 players, and much of this is teen-on-teen crime. Mobile-phone crime figures in London for 2006 showed that:

Keep MP3 players out of sight. Route the headphones inside clothing and consider buying a less distinctive headset.

- *90 per cent of offenders were male and 80 per cent of victims were male*

- *the peak age for offenders was 16*

- *most criminals worked in groups*

Whoever you are, you should consider not only how to carry your electrical goods, but when and where to use them.

Your mobile phone or MP3 player should be kept out of sight in a pocket or bag. Think of it in terms of what it means to the criminal – about £100 on the black market. Therefore take it out and hold it in your hand only if you would be happy to hold a £100 note in the same situation. The ideal spot for either is an internal pocket of a coat or jacket, where a headset can easily reach and you can feel it next to your body. Consider the type of headset you use for either. iPods are equipped with distinctive white headphones. You can buy quality headphones in many colours and styles and should seriously consider what you want to be on show.

PRE-EMPT

Mobiles

All mobiles have voicemail, so there is no requirement to answer a phone just because it's ringing. Speaking on a mobile does two things: it displays what type of phone you have and it reduces your awareness of the environment around you. If you want to use your phone, you can adopt a number of strategies.

Get off the street if you want to make a call. Stop for a coffee or visit a high-street shop. When you make a mobile phone call, you are inevitably less aware of your environment, so ideally you should be where you can observe your surroundings easily. Once you've finished your call, store your phone back in your pocket or bag and continue your journey.

Use hands free; the old 'hard-wired' hands-free kits are ideal. Your phone can remain in your pocket and you can talk while maintaining a decent level of situational awareness. New wireless hands-free kits are very convenient, but consider whether you need to wear one on the high street.

Think before using your mobile phone on the street; you may be distracted from what is happening around or behind you.

Phone tips

When you are out and about, keep your phone on silent alert with the vibrate function turned on. This means you won't draw attention to yourself, and it will encourage you to keep the phone somewhere where you can feel it.

When you first buy a phone, programme it with a pin number for security. Record your phone number, PUK number, PIN number and IMEI number on a piece of paper and keep it somewhere safe (you will find the IMEI number under the battery or by typing *#06# into most handsets). If your phone is stolen, report this information to the police and your service provider and they can bar the phone. You probably won't get the phone back, but at least you know the criminal will get no use out of it either.

If you have children and want them to have a phone for safety, give them your old handset with a new SIM card. They will no doubt protest and want something new, but the chances of them being attacked for your old 'house brick' are limited.

Record your IMEI and PUK/PIN numbers.

MP3 players

When you are listening to any kind of personal music system, your awareness of the world around you disappears. This can be dangerous for a number of reasons, not least if you have to cross a road. Many of you will have an MP3 player to listen to on your

PRE-EMPT

daily commute. This is fine, but following some simple steps will reduce the risk of having it stolen.

Don't listen to music while walking. You are unaware of the environment around you and you will advertise yourself as a victim. When you get on your bus, train or tube, assess where you are sitting and the people around you before you put your MP3 player on. Only then reveal your MP3 player, insert your headphones and start listening, but keep the volume to a level whereby you can still hear normal conversation. Once your journey is complete, finish listening and stow away your headset so it cannot be seen. If you are determined to listen to a stereo while walking or exercising, at least keep the volume to an absolute minimum and understand that, if you forgo your sense of hearing, you need to work especially hard at observing the environment around you to maintain awareness.

Jogging

If you jog, consider the following:

- *Women in particular should consider their clothing. Of course you can wear what you want, but attracting unwanted attention if you're on your own is not sensible.*

- *If possible run with a partner.*

- *If you jog in the dark, choose your route to stay in well-lit areas.*

- *Do not jog at the same time on the same route every day. This is good for your training regime as well as your safety.*

- Consider carrying a bum-bag or similar with your keys, a mobile phone and perhaps a panic alarm. Carrying a mobile phone is useful, not only in the event of a turned-over ankle but also for your own security.

- If you use an MP3 player or digital radio while jogging, understand that you are depriving yourself of your situational awareness.

Women in particular should try to jog with a partner, and should consider choosing clothing that will not attract unwanted attention.

PRE-EMPT

The absolutely key factor in reducing the amount of risk you expose yourself to in all circumstances is improving your observation skills.

The skills involved in driving are a useful example. Any training that you do beyond learning to pass your test will have a common theme; safe driving is 90 per cent observation and 10 per cent skill. Driving at 5mph in the safest NCAP-rated car with the windows painted black will result in an accident. By comparison, driving at 100mph on an open runway where you can see it is clear in all directions for over a mile is a relatively safe experience. Everyday life is the same. If you move about with your 'windows painted black' and don't observe the world around you, the chances are you will be involved in an incident. If you are looking ahead and assessing things as

Help yourself observe the world around you. Wearing hoodies or caps will reduce your peripheral vision and expose you unnecessarily.

you move, the chances are you will spot a problem before you are on top of it. The best way to deal with a problem is to avoid it completely. PRE-EMPT the problem, which enables you to PREVENT your involvement.

People from the West are generally very bad at observing the world and acting accordingly. There are some exceptions to this. For example, off-duty police officers and soldiers develop situational awareness, and it is no coincidence that they are less likely to be the victims of crime. There is no reason you cannot do the same. Initially you may find this an unusual skill to try to learn, but treat it as just that – a skill that can be learned and that will change your life.

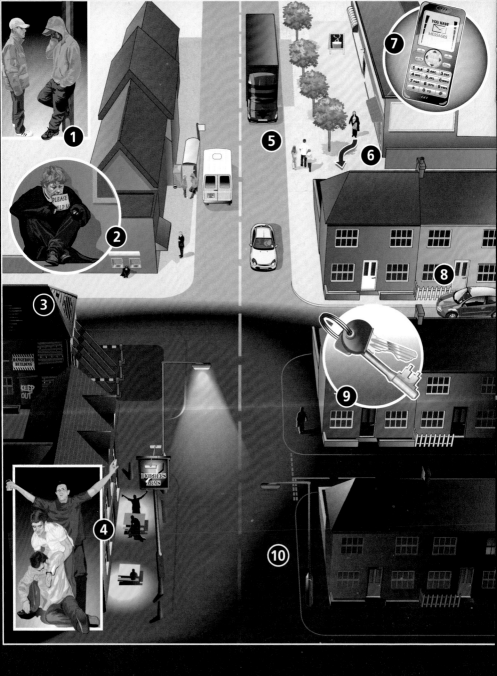

Looking ahead means you can spot places where the pavement might be restricted (1)

Be wary of people hanging around near cashpoints and don't use a cashpoint if it looks unusual (2)

Create space between you and derelict buildings or other places that are used by people sleeping rough (3)

By looking ahead you could avoid this group of drunk young men (4)

Walking facing oncoming traffic provides the best opportunities for observation and safety (5)

Creating space between you and features like alleyways prevents you from being surprised (6)

Rather than using your mobile phone in the street, consider making calls from a shop or café (7)

As you approach your home, you should spot things like people sitting in parked cars (8)

Find your keys before you get to your front door; this means you have something in your hand and can get into your home quickly (9)

If possible, plan to walk in well-lit areas and avoid places like dark alleyways (10)

Commentary

If you are trained on an advanced driving course, you initially use a technique called 'commentary'. This involves saying out loud everything you see while you are driving, specifically any hazards. A hazard could be anything that might cause you to change direction or speed – for example, a junction or bend, or traffic pulling into your path. Giving a running commentary demonstrates to the instructor that you are observing not only the immediate area coming up, but also what is at the limit of visual reference. We will discuss how to use this technique while driving later, but for the moment we will use it as a start point to train ourselves to observe the world around us.

The next time you walk out of your house, play a game and tell yourself everything you are seeing that is relevant to your movement or safety. If approached in the right way, this can actually be a fun activity to do with your partner or children. You will probably feel quite silly to start with, but soon you will find yourself trying to spot more than the person you are with.

Do you really want to use an alleyway like this on the way home? Plan your route to maximise your ability to observe the environment.

PRE-EMPT

Get used to doing this on a routine basis and you will probably notice a number of interesting side effects:

- *Places that you thought were familiar will suddenly contain things you have not seen before. You might ask yourself whether they have always been there and how you missed them.*

- *Your senses will thank you for using them and become more active. The more you look and listen, the more detail you will perceive.*

- *You will naturally start to make decisions about your actions. You may even change your routes so you have a better view of things like openings to alleyways or you might keep away from dark areas of a street.*

Observation links

Once you find you can comfortably walk down a street while talking yourself through what you see, you can move on to the next stage, which is creating 'observation links' in your mind. This can simply be thought of as asking 'so what' when you identify something of interest. If we return to the driving comparison, here are some examples of observation links:

- **You see a tractor in a field ahead.** *Ask yourself 'so what?' You conclude that there might be mud on the road and therefore you reduce your speed.*

- **Approaching a corner, you see a set of goalposts just off the road.** *Ask yourself 'so what?' You conclude that, as it is a Saturday, there are likely to be children playing in the area, so you reduce your speed.*

Absence of the normal and presence of the abnormal

The final stage of developing your situational awareness – becoming familiar with what normality looks like – should happen naturally as you start to observe more about the environment you live in. This skill relates both to the fixed environment (the buildings, rubbish bins, street furniture and trees) and to the activity within it (the people, vehicles and animals). Once you are familiar with the feel of normality, you can look for the two key indicators that something is wrong:

An open window could mean the owner is airing the house, but it could also be the entrance point for an ongoing burglary.

- the absence of the normal

- the presence of the abnormal

This is a technique that has been used successfully by security forces for many years and is taught specifically to soldiers employed on counter-insurgency campaigns. You will already do it to some extent automatically, as it is an instinctive skill we all possess. An interesting use of this natural ability can be seen in animal trackers. Many say that they don't actually look for animal signs; rather, they allow themselves to become aware of the environment and let their subconscious draw the eye to what has been changed – that is, what is no longer 'normal'. Here are some examples that relate to everyday experiences.

PRE-EMPT

Absence of the normal

- **In a busy bar, everyone has a drink except the two men immediately behind your partner.** *This is absence of the normal. They may be waiting for a friend, or they could be looking for someone a little the worse for wear to pickpocket.*

- **In a car park you park next to a van that is missing the rear number plate.** *This is absence of the normal. It may have fallen off and the driver has yet to notice, or it could be that the vehicle is stolen or being used for criminal activity.*

Presence of the abnormal

- **While walking down your street on a cold winter's day, you notice the downstairs window of a house wide open.** *This is presence of the abnormal. It could mean the owner is airing the house, but it could also be the entrance point for an ongoing burglary.*

- **While driving, you pull up at traffic lights next to a brand-new Range Rover and it is being driven by a very young male.** *This is presence of the abnormal. He may be very wealthy or driving his parents' car, but it could also be that he is a car thief.*

Once you get used to these three techniques – ***commentary, observation links, and looking for the absence of the normal or the presence of the abnormal*** – you will find that you start to consider your actions in far greater detail. By using these generic observation methods you can improve your situational awareness in any environment.

CHAPTER TWO

Driving

B y far the most dangerous activity that most people will ever be involved in is driving a car. While you are more likely to be slightly injured during a mugging or assault, the risk from being seriously injured or killed is highest from a road-traffic accident. The Road Casualties in Great Britain main results published in 2006 show that there were:

- *280,840 reported casualties on the roads of whom*

  - *3,221 were killed*

  - *31,130 were seriously injured*

Compare this with the 859 cases of homicide in the UK (many of which were criminal on criminal) over the same period, and you can see that getting into your vehicle is a high-risk activity.

One of the aims of this book is to allow you to make your own threat assessments based on a greater understanding of the risks you are actually exposed to. As explained in the Introduction, this book does not set out to deal with the 'knife fighting a Russian barman' scenario. Instead it concentrates on what is most likely to

PRE-EMPT

affect you. There is no doubt that you are most at risk from a road-traffic accident.

You are far more likely to be killed or seriously injured in your car than in a terrorist attack. It is relatively easy to manage this risk.

If you really want to reduce the risk that you and your family are exposed to in everyday life, the start point has to be driving. None of us likes to think we are bad drivers, and men in particular tend to hold a significantly inflated opinion of their own skills. Put your pride to one side for a moment and ask yourself whether you've actually been taught anything that you are sure is correct since you passed your test. The majority of the UK population have not. Accepting that you may have something to learn is the first step towards keeping you and your loved ones a lot safer.

The best way to improve your safety on the road is to attend some form of further driver training. When we 'learn to drive', we do very little learning about how to drive and a lot of learning about how to pass the test. Most of us actually learn to drive by making small mistakes over the following two or three years and developing habits that we find effective.

There is a wide variety of organisations and individuals providing further training, but by far the most established and recognised is the Institute of Advanced Motorists. You will find its details in the list of Websites and Sources of Further Information. In addition to learning about driving, you can also get a qualification that will earn you a discount on your car insurance – very useful indeed. If you would rather do your own study, then consider reading *Roadcraft: The Police Drivers' Handbook*, which is produced by the Home Office.

Most of the UK driving population have received no instruction beyond passing their test. Take the opportunity to learn how to drive.

PRE-EMPT

Once again we are going to use the three techniques of commentary, observation links and looking for the absence of the normal or presence of the abnormal.

Commentary

In your own car you can get away with talking to yourself without feeling too silly, so the first exercise to improve your driving is to start describing all the hazards that you can see. Try to look not only in the area immediately in front of your car but also to the visible extent of the road ahead. On a busy high street this may only be 20 metres ahead, but on a motorway it could be over a mile. As you look forward, start saying out loud all the potential hazards you can see. This includes anything that might cause you to change direction or adjust your speed.

Observation links

Commentary is a very useful exercise to conduct on your own or with someone else in the car. If you have children or friends who have recently learned how to drive, this is a great thing to do while you are driving and they are in the car. If you are a more experienced driver, you will

You see a **building site near the road.** ASK YOURSELF 'SO WHAT'? *You conclude there might be mud on the road and therefore you reduce your speed.*

naturally 'see' more than they do. Once you are able to give a running commentary on what you are seeing, start then to ask yourself 'so what?' and come up with some 'observation links'.

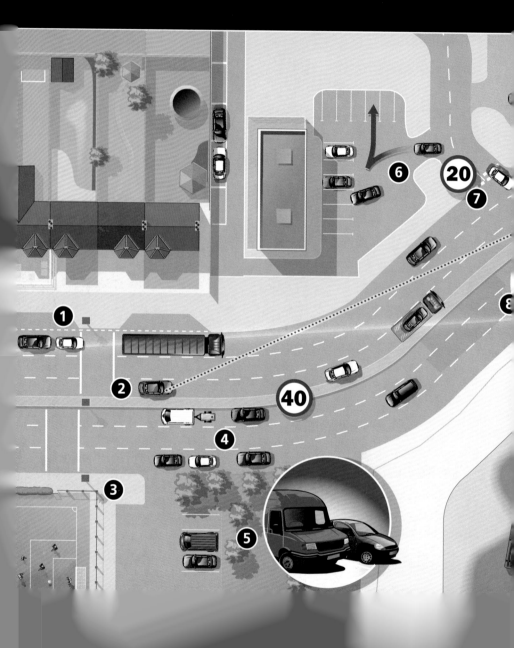

1. The 'bump and jack' can happen at traffic lights, T-junctions or roundabouts

2. Positioning the car on the outside of a bend allows for best observation

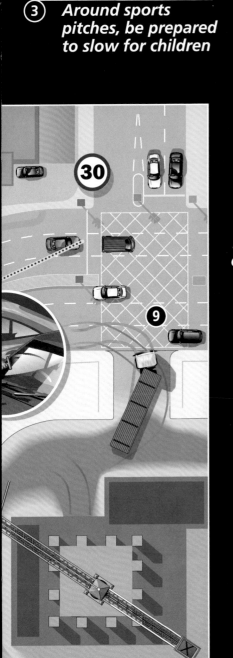

(3) **Around sports pitches, be prepared to slow for children**

(4) Watch your distance. When moving remember 'only a fool breaks the 2-second rule'; stop so that you can see 'tyres on tarmac'

(5) Avoid parking next to vans or the stairwells in multistorey car parks, and in places that can't be seen by passers-by

(6) Reversing into spaces not only means it's easier and quicker to drive away; it also allows you to observe the area before getting out of your car

(7) Speed is a key contributing factor in many accidents; keep to a safe limit

(8) Roll up to junctions rather than stopping and if possible pick the middle lane to create a space between you and windscreen-washers or traders

(9) Be prepared to slow for mud on roads around building sites or exits from farmers' fields

Absence of the normal or presence of the abnormal

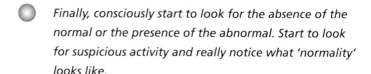 *Finally, consciously start to look for the absence of the normal or the presence of the abnormal. Start to look for suspicious activity and really notice what 'normality' looks like.*

Many people will find these exercises quite challenging to begin with. As you start to notice in detail what is happening in the road in front of you, you may find that you cannot speak quickly enough to say out loud everything you see. Many of you will find you are driving much more slowly than you normally would in order to get everything out. Whatever you do, please drive safely while you try these exercises.

DRIVING SKILLS

Positioning

Now you are observing a little more about the road in front, you can start to position your vehicle to get a better view of the conditions, environment and activity. This is a subject of significant depth and complexity; however, in simple terms, maximise the use of your side of the road so you give yourself the best opportunity to react.

While driving in town or at low speed there is less to be gained from positioning. However, you should still think about where exactly you want to place the car. In particular, it is good practice to position yourself correctly when turning right and at the approach to roundabouts.

Positioning takes on far more importance when you are on the

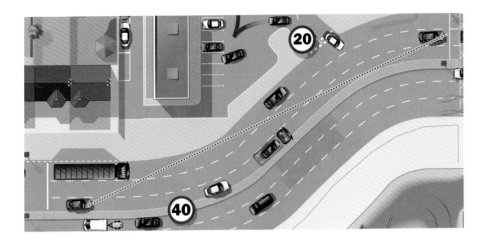

outside of a bend, while remaining on your side of the road. This achieves two things. First, it ensures that you are getting the best possible vantage point to observe the road ahead. Secondly, by driving on the outside of the bend you are making it less sharp, which gives you a smoother ride; at higher speeds it also allows you to move through the bend more quickly and safely.

Positioning yourself on the outside of the bend gives you increased observation and a smoother ride.

Try this when you are next out. You will find that by approaching a bend on the outside of your own lane you are able to see far better what is around the next corner.

Driving defensively

Once you have improved your observation skills and learned how to position your car to maximise both your observation and your chance of reacting, you can then think about how best to drive defensively. Rather than being the mastery of any particular skill, driving defensively is a state of mind that aims to minimise risk. Here are some simple guidelines:

● *Assume that all other road users are incompetent and expect them to do something stupid.*

Driving

- Always allow an ample space between you and the car in front, at least 2 seconds. Pick a point that the car in front passes and then say out loud 'only a fool breaks the 2-second rule'. You should be able to say it before your car passes the same point.

- When you stop, maintain a sensible distance from the  car in front to allow you to pull out if necessary. A good guideline is to ensure you can see rear 'tyres on tarmac'; say it out loud to start with.

- Make yourself visible. Driving with sidelights on is compulsory in some European countries. At sunrise and sunset keep your dipped headlights on. Ensure you indicate where appropriate to let other road users know your intention.

If you master these skills, you will already be managing the risks you are exposed to in a much better way. The next step is dovetailing in some behaviours that will increase your security.

We will start from the basics of getting in and out of your car.

CAR SKILLS

Getting into your car

Some 20 per cent of car crime in the UK happens in car parks, with hospitals and railway stations being statistically the most dangerous places to park. Before you get to you car, have your keys in your hand. This means you need to start getting them out of your pocket or bag a good 50–100 metres away. By holding

PRE-EMPT

them in your dominant hand, you will not only speed up your entry into the car, but also have something to defend yourself with should someone try to approach you. As you get near your vehicle, observe the area around it. Are there people nearby? Are the windows intact? Is there anything under your car? For example, if a group of young men is sitting in the car next to yours and they look suspicious, walk past and ask the parking attendant or someone else to escort you to your car.

Do not disarm your remote alarm from 30 metres away. Wait until you are next to the driver's door, then get in quickly and lock the doors. Practise doing this with your children as a game. When sitting in a stationary vehicle you are vulnerable. The aim should be to sort out yourself and others in the car quickly, do up seatbelts and move off as soon as possible. If you do this every time, it becomes routine. To help with this you may want to consider reversing into parking bays rather than 'nosey parking'. This means you have a better field of observation when you return to your car and can leave quickly if necessary.

Criminals target car parks. Think ahead when returning to your car. No one feels comfortable rummaging for their keys in a deserted car park.

Getting out of your car

When you arrive at a parking spot and reverse into it, your doors should be locked and windows already shut. Once you have turned the engine off and everyone has their seatbelt off, unlock the doors, exit the vehicle quickly, lock it again and leave. This sounds the height of simplicity, but many of us spend a significant amount of time with doors open and keys in the ignition while getting out of our cars. This presents a golden opportunity to anyone who wants a vehicle. If you are arriving home, or need to open a door once you get out of your car, ensure you have the correct key in your hand before you open the vehicle door. This again can be used as a weapon if required. Sometimes when you arrive home it will be necessary to do a significant amount of loading or unloading. If you are on your own, consider whether you need to do it all or whether you can wait for someone to help.

If you have children, the best solution is to have someone with you to help you unload shopping.

If you have been shopping on your own, you can put the fridge and freezer items in bags on your front seat and the dry goods in the boot. When you get home, park with the doors locked, gather up the items on your front seat, quickly leave the car and get into your home in one action. This reduces the time you would otherwise spend on your own with your house and car unlocked.

Getting in and out of your car quickly and efficiently is of course difficult to achieve if you have children in car seats or items in the boot. You are more likely to be approached if you are on your own, so having someone with you to help will always be the best solution. In any situation, if you feel uncomfortable, it is best to keep observing, and if someone does approach you, make him or her aware that you feel uncomfortable. It is always good to have a panic alarm and mobile phone to hand.

PRE-EMPT

Planning to stop

You are most at risk in a car when you are stationary. This is also the time you are likely to be approached by windscreen-washers, flower-sellers, street beggars, etc. If possible, plan where you are going to stop in advance. If you are observing ahead and see lights change, slow down early to reduce the amount of time you actually spend stationary. If you get good at this, you can slowly roll up and always keep your vehicle edging forward. If there are three lanes available, try to get in the middle one, as it is more difficult for pedestrians to approach you there.

Finally, when you are approaching a location where you will have to stop, look for an escape route and leave yourself enough room to manoeuvre to it. There is no need to pull away with your wheels spinning as in a Hollywood movie if you feel threatened. A moving car with locked doors and closed windows is extremely difficult for a pedestrian to get into or stop. Looking for an escape route also encourages you to notice what is around you once you have stopped.

When approaching a junction, roll up slowly and choose a safe route to escape through if necessary.

Consider your personal safety while driving. You should always have the doors locked and the windows closed. All belongings should be out of view and if possible in the boot. Obviously this is sometimes tremendously difficult, particularly for young families, so it is worth considering the use of tinted back windows.

Think about what you do and don't need to carry in your car. A suggested car kit is listed opposite and easily fits in a small plastic storage box from a DIY store. Ensure it is secured in your boot with elastic bungees, available from stores like Halfords.

Tinted windows allow you to leave items in the back of a car without tempting thieves.

Then place a large blanket on top of the box, either to sit on in the summer or to act as a duvet should you be stuck in the winter. Other items to consider include a torch, additional warm clothing and a large umbrella, so that, if you do break down, you have some protection from the elements.

PRE-EMPT

Everyone should carry a car safety box

- jump leads
- tow rope
- warning triangle
- top-up bottle of oil
- small first-aid kit and rubber gloves
- 2-litre bottle of drinking water

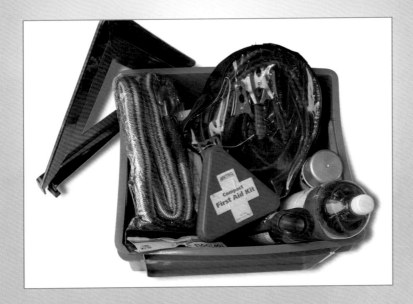

Carjacking is a worrying trend that is on the increase. There were over 10,000 carjackings in the UK in 2005, which is approximately 4 per cent of all vehicle theft. The most commonly targeted vehicles are BMW, Porsche, Mercedes and Jaguar, and many are chosen well in advance – for example, specific types of Mercedes are often targeted for the African taxi market.

Two main factors contribute to the rise in carjackings. First, improvements in car security systems make it more difficult for thieves to steal an unattended car. Secondly, criminals have realised that, for a limited extra risk, they are able to gain not only a vehicle complete with keys and immobiliser fob, but also the personal belongings of the victim.

The most worrying possibility for victims of a carjacking is that they will be taken to a secondary location for a violent or sexual assault.

Carjacking most commonly occurs while the victim is entering or exiting a parked vehicle, so your drills for approaching, getting

Entering or exiting from a parked car is when you are most likely to be carjacked. Ensure you remain aware of the environment around you.

PRE-EMPT

into and leaving your vehicle are very important. Often the crime happens near to home, because the vehicle has been identified and followed. In addition to car parks, it can occur at stop points like traffic lights and crossings, but this is less common.

The standard car entry and exit drills we discussed earlier will ensure you are a difficult target for the carjacker, but it is also worth considering in detail where to park your car. Leaving your car in a well-lit location that is manned or monitored by CCTV is ideal, but also consider the vehicles you park next to. Don't park next to vans or groups of men, and try to avoid the spot immediately next to the stairwell in a multistorey car park.

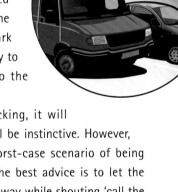

If you are the victim of a carjacking, it will happen quickly and your reaction will be instinctive. However, your aim should be to avoid the worst-case scenario of being taken to a secondary crime scene. The best advice is to let the criminal have the vehicle and to run away while shouting 'call the police' or 'fire' (these get more attention than shouting 'help'). Of course it is your decision, but if your instinct is to act against the criminal, then you must be decisive. See Chapter 8 for advice.

If you are already in the vehicle and asked to drive somewhere, you need to act. There is no pleasant reason for you to be taken to a second location. Consider either running at a natural stop point like traffic lights or crashing at low speed at a well-lit and populated location while you can. Mentally prepare for what is going to happen. If you're going to run, then check whether the doors are locked. Are you wearing your seatbelt? Visually check both and make a plan. If you decide to crash your car, do you have air bags? Keep your arms away from the centre of the steering wheel. Is your seatbelt tight? Is your door unlocked? Whichever option you choose, once the vehicle has stopped, get out and run while shouting for attention.

Another possible way for criminals to effect a carjack is the 'bump and jack'. A vehicle will bump into the rear of your car while you are stationary at lights or a junction. Most of us will then find

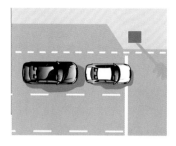

a spot to pull over, inspect the damage and exchange insurance details. While you are out of the vehicle, the passenger of the other car will steal yours, and then both cars will be driven away. The nightmare scenario, of course, is that you have children strapped into the vehicle. If you are involved in a minor accident and you are concerned about the other vehicle involved, particularly if it has two or more male occupants, then there is nothing wrong with staying in your car with the doors locked and the window slightly ajar so you can speak.

If you are happy to get out of your car, write down the registration of the other vehicle, its colour and type before you get out. At least that way you have it in your pocket should things go wrong. If you are still unhappy after talking to the other person involved, then call the police and ask them to attend. Someone who has genuinely bumped into the back of your vehicle will understand, even if he or she is not entirely delighted with having to wait for the police. If he or she drives off, ensure you get the details of the vehicle and a description of the occupants. If someone becomes violent or aggressive, then drive off and call the police as soon as you can to let them know you have left the scene of an accident.

Remember, if you really want to improve your personal safety, by far the best thing you can do is to improve your driving. This chapter can only be an introduction to a vast and complex subject. Do consider getting further training from a recognised supplier. And please drive safely.

PRE-EMPT

CHAPTER THREE

First Aid and Fire

There are some things we should all know, like the number to dial in an emergency. We learn most of these at school, but unfortunately some essentials are not on the curriculum. Having an idea of basic first aid and what to do in the event of a fire are two life skills that sadly not all people possess. The chances are that, if you live to a healthy age, you will experience a situation in which you will need either to use some basic first aid or to deal with an unintended fire.

FIRST AID

Figures published in 2006 state that over 13,000 people die in everyday accidents in the UK every year. In many cases the life could have been saved if someone with first-aid knowledge had been at hand. In terms of cost-benefit analysis, the basics of first aid can be learned in about 5 minutes and could save the life of your most precious loved one. If you have children and no first-aid training, then you should strongly consider what you will do when inevitably your child injures him or herself. It is of course up to you to decide whether it is worth taking the time to learn some basic first-aid skills.

We all have a moral and in some cases legal responsibility to treat people in the way we would like to be treated; this includes helping someone who might be injured. There are a number of scare stories about people being sued by victims after they have tried to help them. This is a rare and unfortunate occurrence, and my advice is that your moral compass should guide you to provide assistance if it is safe for you to do so. In the UK we normally say that this is a concern, but actually no one has been sued to date. There is the 'Good Samaritan' law in Europe, which says that, if you offer first aid with good intention, you are OK.

There are many providers of first-aid training. In the UK the British Red Cross runs a variety of first-aid courses that are invaluable and enjoy-

*You should know how to look after your children, not if but **when** they hurt themselves.*

able. If you need it for your work, you may find that your employer will be happy to pay for you to attend a course.

I have teamed up with the British Red Cross to provide the best first-aid advice. You will find details of its website in the list of Websites and Sources of Further Information.

PRE-EMPT

How to deal with an emergency

- Keep calm and look for any dangers to yourself or to the injured person.

- Find out what happened and how.

- How many casualties are there?

- Is there anyone around who can help you?

- Do you need an ambulance?

- Assess the injured person.

- Check for a response to see if they are conscious.

- Check that the airway is open.

- Check for breathing.

When there is more than one injured person, go to the quiet one first. They may be unconscious and need immediate attention.

For an unconscious person

Open the airway. Place one hand on the forehead and gently tilt the head back and lift the chin. Use two fingers on the point of the chin to lift the chin.

Check breathing. Look, listen and feel for breathing for no more than 10 seconds. Look for chest movement, listen for sound and feel for breath on your cheek.

Emergency first-aid techniques _____

Resuscitation (adult)

If the person is not breathing normally, you must call an ambulance then start cardio-pulmonary resuscitation (CPR), which is a combination of chest compressions and rescue breaths.

1. *Place your hands on the centre of their chest and, with the heel of your hand press down (4–5cm). After every 30 chest compressions give 2 breaths.*
2. *Open the airway. Place one hand on the forehead, and gently tilt the head back and lift the chin. Pinch the person's nose. Place your mouth over their mouth and – by blowing steadily – attempt 2 rescue breaths each over 1 second.*
3. *Continue with cycles of 30 chest compressions and 2* rescue breaths until emergency help arrives or the person begins to breathe normally. If you are unable or unwilling to give rescue breaths, just give chest compressions.

Resuscitation (child 1 year old to puberty)

If a child is not breathing, and you are alone, give 1 minute of CPR then call an ambulance. If another person is present, ask them to call an ambulance straight away, then begin CPR.

1. *Open the airway. Place one hand on the forehead, and gently tilt the head back and lift the chin. Remove any visible obstructions from the mouth and nose.*
2. *Pinch the child's nose. Place your mouth over the child's mouth and attempt 5 initial rescue breaths.*
3. *Place your hands on the centre of their chest and, with the heel of your hand, press down*

one-third of the depth of the chest using one or two hands, depending on the size of the child in relation to you. After every 30 chest compressions give 2 breaths.

4. Continue with cycles of 30 chest compressions and 2 rescue breaths until emergency help arrives or the child begins to breathe normally.

Resuscitation (baby 0–1 year old)

If a baby is not breathing, and you are alone, give 1 minute of CPR then take the baby with you when you call an ambulance. If another person is present, ask them to call an ambulance straight away, then begin CPR.

▲ 1. Open the airway. Place one hand on the forehead and gently tilt the head back and lift the chin. Remove any visible obstructions from the mouth and nose.

▲ 2. Place your mouth over the mouth and nose of the baby and – by blowing steadily – attempt 5 initial rescue breaths.

◄ 3. Place 2 fingers in the middle of the chest and press down one-third of the depth of the chest. After 30 chest compressions give 2 breaths.

4. Continue with cycles of 30 chest compressions and 2 rescue breaths until emergency help arrives or the baby begins to breathe.

55

Recovery position (adult/child)

If an adult or child is unconscious but breathing, place them on their side in the recovery position. This is a safe and comfortable position for them.

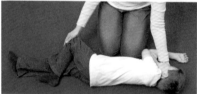

1. *Place arm nearest you at a right angle, with palm facing up.*
2. *Move other arm, and place back of hand against the person's cheek. Then get hold of knee furthest from you and pull up until foot is flat on the floor.*
3. *Pull the knee towards you keeping the person's hand pressed against their cheek, and position the leg at a right angle.*
4. *Make sure that the airway remains open by tilting the head back and lifting the chin, and check breathing.*
5. *Monitor the casualty's condition until help arrives.*

Recovery position (baby)

If a baby is unconscious but breathing, hold them on their side, head tilted, as if you were giving them a cuddle, with their head lower than their tummy.

Choking (adult and child)

If someone is unable to speak, cough or breathe:

1. *Give up to 5 back blows between the shoulder blades with the heel of your hand.*
2. *Check the mouth quickly after each one and remove any obvious obstruction.*

If the obstruction is still present:

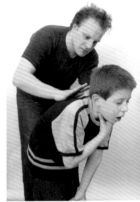

3. *Give up to 5 abdominal thrusts. Place a clenched fist above the navel and pull inwards and upwards. Check the mouth quickly after each one. If the obstruction does not clear after three cycles of back blows and abdominal thrusts dial **999** (or **112**) for an ambulance.*
4. *Continue until help arrives and resuscitate if necessary.*

If you deliver abdominal thrusts, ensure the casualty visits a doctor.

Choking (baby)

If a baby is unable to breathe, cough or cry:

1. *Give up to 5 back blows between the shoulder blades with the heel of your hand.*
2. *Check the mouth quickly after each one and remove any obvious obstruction.*

If the obstruction is still present:

3. *Give up to 5 chest thrusts. With two fingers in the middle of the chest, push inwards and upwards. Check the mouth quickly after each one. If the obstruction does not clear after three cycles of back blows and chest thrusts dial **999** (or **112**) for an ambulance.*
4. *Continue until help arrives and resuscitate if necessary.*

Burns and scalds

Burns and scalds are among the most common injuries requiring emergency treatment in the UK.

1. *Cool the burn as quickly as possible by placing the affected area under cold running water for at least 10 minutes.*
2. *Raise the limb to reduce swelling.*
3. *Cover the injury using a clean pad or cling film, and seek medical advice. Dial **999** (or **112**) in severe cases.*

The British Red Cross offers a wide range of first-aid training courses, from two to twenty-eight hours. Whether you just want to learn some first-aid skills to feel prepared in case of an accident or need an HSE-approved course for your workplace, we can help. Our trainers have hands-on experience that they draw upon to bring the subject to life. The atmosphere on courses is friendly and relaxed, and our trainers are very approachable and happy to answer your questions.

To find out more, visit **redcross.org.uk/firstaid**, call the national first aid helpline on **0870 170 9222** or email **firstaid@redcross.org.uk**.

We may live in the twenty-first century, but fire remains a significant risk to life, even in the developed world. Each year in the UK there are around 68,000 house fires, in which around 400 people die and 13,800 are injured.

Even if you make it out of a home fire alive, it will destroy every precious item you own.

1 *Ensure the whole family knows where the first-aid box is kept and how to use the contents*

2 *Keeping a house fire plan on the fridge will ensure your children and perhaps house guests are aware of anything specific to your home*

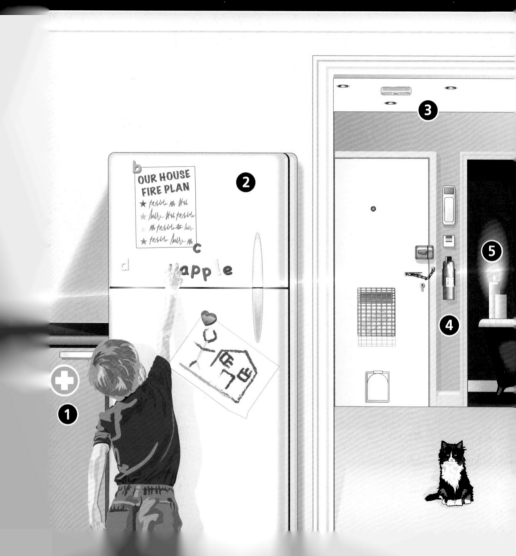

OUR HOUSE FIRE PLAN

apple

(3) *Ensure you have smoke detectors and that the batteries are changed regularly*

(4) *Keeping a fire extinguisher by the front door keeps fire safety in mind*

(5) *Do not leave candles unattended*

(6) *A fire blanket can cost as little as £15 and it will last for the rest of your life*

(7) *Most house fires are caused by electrical faults; keep your appliances well serviced*

(8) *Ensure you know how to deal with a pan fire or oven fire*

The government produces a very good guide called *The Fire Prevention Handbook*; you can order a copy free online or download it in a PDF format. This publication is ideal to have readily available at home and discuss with your children or other people in your home.

The basics of what to do in the event of a fire are simple: if you experience a fire, no matter how small, get everyone out of the building and dial 999. You should attempt to fight a fire only if it is safe for you to do so and after you have alerted others to evacuate the building.

The best way to fight fire is to prevent it. Sensible use of electricity, candles and in particular cooking appliances will prevent most home fires. Twenty people every day are killed or injured in kitchen fires.

Think carefully about any celebrations you are planning, and if you buy any fireworks, ensure they conform to BS 7114 and that you produce a plan for how you will use them. If you do smoke, ensure your burning ash is disposed of safely. Someone dies every three days in a cigarette fire.

How to deal with a pan fire

- **DO NOT** take any risks – get everyone out and call 999
- turn off the heat if it is safe to do so
- place a fire blanket over the pan
- leave to cool
- do not throw water on the pan
- do not use a fire extinguisher

Take sensible precautions to deal with fire. First and most important, ensure you know how to escape from your home and working environment. This applies just as much when you are staying in a hotel or visiting an office block: take the time to find out where the fire exits are and any alternative routes you may have. At home ensure you think about what you might do if you are stuck on the first floor and whether you should have a safe room with a fire door where you can wait for the fire service. If you have children, consider keeping a 'what to do in the event of a fire' sheet in a prominent place – for example, on the fridge door.

If you buy fireworks to use yourself, ensure they comply with BS advice; but you might prefer to take your family to an organised display.

Ensure you have adequate equipment in your home. As an absolute minimum, you should fit smoke detectors on every floor. Of the 470 deaths resulting from house fires each year, an average of 270 occur where there is no smoke detector present, and in a further 90 cases the smoke detector does not work. The lesson is clear. Check that your detectors work on a regular basis and consider whether it is time to upgrade old sensors to a new system. Keeping a fire blanket in your kitchen and a fire extinguisher in your downstairs hall means you have a good chance of preventing any small problem developing into a catastrophe.

Fire and people

If your clothes are on fire, you should **STOP**, **DROP** and **ROLL**. The natural instinct of many people is to run, which of course makes the problem worse. If you see this happening, try to 'encourage' the person to the floor.

If someone's clothes are on fire and he is panicking, you may need to use force to get him to the floor.

PRE-EMPT

PREVENT

Part
Two

CHAPTER FOUR

Western Crime

T his chapter covers the types of crime you are probably most concerned about – those that involve the potential for harm to you or to someone you care about. Whether the criminal wants to take some of your belongings, enter your home or attempt a carjacking, the common theme is a commitment to use violence if necessary to achieve the aim. There are differences in the threats that you might encounter from city to city and country to country; however, the basic information is relevant wherever you are.

Statistically speaking, we will all be affected by a violent crime at some point during our lives, and that makes this the most relevant chapter for us all.

AVOIDING VIOLENT CRIME

Violent crime statistics

In 2006 the UK crime statistics were in general down on those for 1995 (which are used as a baseline for comparison). However, they still reflect a society where violence is part of the landscape.

Figures published in 2006 show that in England and Wales in 2005 there were:

- 2,412,000 violent crimes against the individual, of which
  - 57,7000 were wounding
  - 25,5000 were robbery

- 92,000 snatches from the person

- 492,000 stealth thefts from the person

- 214,000 thefts of a vehicle

- 1,210,000 thefts from a vehicle

If you do not take responsibility for your own personal security, at some point during your life you will be one of these statistics. Now is the time to learn how to reduce that risk.

When and where does violence occur?

Crime is ubiquitous in the UK and probably always will be. Whether you are in an inner-city estate with a drugs and violence culture, or taking your dog for a walk in the English countryside, there are always crime risks to be considered. It is possible to identify trends, and it will come as no surprise that a significant proportion of violent crimes occurs at the weekends in city centres. It is also known that much of the serious violence occurs 'criminal on criminal', so the risk of an unprovoked violent crime is extremely low. However, like a good boy scout, 'be prepared' and maintain a constant level of vigilance.

In the UK there have been a number of high-profile court cases involving 'motiveless violence'. This needs to be quantified. The phenomenon of 'happy slapping' is the best example of 'motiveless

PREVENT

violence'. In a typical incident, a group will look for a suitable victim and then film each other with mobile telephone cameras conducting their attack. There are similar types of crime involving assaults on street dwellers. (The best way to deal with such an attack is discussed in Chapter 8.) While the criminals in this instance have no ultimate goal and are therefore 'motiveless', they will go through some form of selection process to choose a victim. I am going to help you influence this selection process.

In general terms, for someone to attack you he or she will either want something from you or will have taken a dislike to you because of your actions. You can reduce the risk of either of these things happening. In the worst case, when the motive is tenuous, you can ensure you are prepared and ready to act.

Alcohol

A large proportion of violent crime has one single cause: alcohol. The UK Government statistics published in 2006 reveal that 40 per cent of violent crimes, 78 per cent of assaults and 88 per cent of criminal damage cases were committed while the offender was under the influence of alcohol. Another figure of note is that 16–24-year-old men

are far more likely than any other demographic group to be involved in violent crime – about 16 per cent of this group every year.

Identifying people who are under the influence of alcohol, and particularly young men, is a good first step to avoiding confrontation. Of course, most people are able to control themselves in these circumstances, and many young men are utterly charming when they've had a drink. It is, however, sensible to be aware of the potential actions of these groups if you want to stay safe.

Some of you will take the opinion that the next logical step is to stay away from areas that are likely to contain young, drunk men.

In purely statistical terms, it is fair to say a significant proportion of violent crimes happen between drunk young men.

This would probably include any town or city centre on a weekend or evening. There is no doubt that this will reduce risk, but a restriction of your freedom has to be seen as a victory for the criminal.

Your local police force will apply significant resources to your town centre at the weekends, so perhaps a more sensible compromise is to ensure you are fully aware of your surroundings if you do decide to venture out for some evening entertainment. This includes moderating your own alcohol consumption so you are always able to decide when to leave a situation that is deteriorating or to detect if your own drink has been interfered with.

If you are out with friends, an ideal way to ensure that someone is able to make a decision in your group is to designate a driver. At the height of the Irish Troubles, British soldiers out socialising were required to have one of their party remain sober and observe the reactions of others. This person was referred to as 'shark watch'. Frequently, he would identify that some of the locals were becoming agitated or perhaps that one of his own group had had a little too much and should be escorted back to barracks. While you probably won't want to employ such a formal arrangement, a designated driver does provide a sober and sensible safety blanket for an evening's activity. Groups of girls enjoying a night out should strongly consider having one sober member in their party.

In a busy bar, always ensure that you can see your drink.

PREVENT

Bars

We have already identified that alcohol has a direct link with violent crime. When busy, bars present a crowded situation where observation can be limited and potential courses of action restricted. In all respects bars hold potential dangers, and you should consider a few simple things while you are out.

Before a night out, when you are thinking about what to wear, decide exactly what you are going to take. Remember the advice given already in Chapter 1 about carrying your belongings.

As soon as you get to an unfamiliar bar, visually locate the fire and other exits. Ensure that you visit the toilets as soon as you can, and on the way have a look around. (Doing this immediately also means you are likely to miss out on buying the first round of drinks!) This way you can locate any rear exits and also have a quick look at who else is in the bar. Do you want to stay if you were followed in by a group of football supporters in red shirts and at the back

of the room is a large group of football supporters in blue shirts?

It can be surprisingly easy to spot people who will annoy each other.

The golden rule of drinking is to be able to see your drink from the moment it leaves the bar staff's hand to the moment you finish it. If you cannot see it because you are in the toilet and leave it with someone else, or someone else is buying you a drink, make sure you trust that person. If you cannot see it because you've drunk too much, it's probably time to leave anyway. In busy places, or where you feel there might be more danger of your drink being interfered with, drink from a bottle, and if you are really concerned, then keep your thumb on top of the bottle. Women who might be particularly conscious of the risk should avoid where possible drinking from pint glasses, as they offer a large target for people to drop something into. Obviously, women should not accept drinks from people they do not know.

Drinking to a point where you are unable to look after yourself is irresponsible – also, it is just not fun.

As we discussed earlier, it is irresponsible to drink to the point that you are unable to make a decision about your own safety. If you are unable to look after yourself, you can expect to be a victim of crime and you will have little grounds to complain about it; losing control is unforgivable. If you are female, you have to accept the fact that you are particularly vulnerable. Any way you look at it, drinking to the point where decision making is impossible is a bad idea. You stop enjoying yourself and you immediately set yourself up as a victim.

Unfortunately, after years of questioning, all the doctors I know have come up with the same answer on drinking: there is no magic way to sober up if you've had too much. The only sensible advice is to ensure you are fully hydrated and to drink water or some other soft drink if you start to feel that you may have drunk too much. Better still, drink water or soft drinks throughout the night interspersed with alcohol. In many East European nations, vodka is followed by water. By doing this you can control much more easily how much you've had to drink, and the morning-after effects are significantly reduced. Those who have travelled extensively will be able to confirm that the UK drinking 'routine' is unique, and not something to be particularly proud of. Anything you can do to slow your consumption and increase your alertness will improve the quality of your evening and benefit your security.

Throughout the night your valuables should remain with you at all times. This can be challenging during the winter if you have a coat and there is no cloakroom. The only sensible option if you do have to make a pile of jackets is to ensure you keep any valuable belongings on your person.

As mentioned earlier in this chapter in connection with alcohol-fuelled crime, most situations are made safer by having a designated driver with you.

PREVENT

Finally, the worst situation that you will be exposed to in a bar is being assaulted, or becoming involved in an assault that occurs near you. In almost all circumstances bar fights are very easy to predict. The amount of posturing and chest puffing that goes on between groups of young men before one or other will finally decide to act should give you a good indication that something is about to happen. You will find some simple information on how to deal physically with these situations in Chapter 8, but the best advice is to move elsewhere in the bar or, better still, leave and drink somewhere else if you feel aggravation developing. If you have somehow become the source of frustration, always bow out gracefully. It really does take more courage to walk away than it does to stay and get involved. The chances are that, whatever the disagreement is about, it is not worth spending the rest of your night in casualty or a police cell.

Getting home

When walking back to your house or arriving home in a car, it is worth considering all the steps involved in entering your house. Remember, when you are going into your house, you have the door open and your back to the street. This is something that can be exploited by opportunist thieves. Entry and exit to your home from your car are discussed in the next section, so here we will consider what to do if you are on foot.

When approaching your home, ensure you have the right key to hand.

When walking up to your house, have your keys ready and in your hand. There are a number of ways to use a set of keys or everyday item to protect yourself; these are discussed in Chapter 8. When approaching your home, hold your keys with the key-ring end in the palm of your dominant hand, with the sharp end of the keys running along your thumb.

As you approach the house, use your observation skills and have a good look around. Ensure everything looks normal. If you think there is someone acting suspiciously or if you see evidence to suggest that your home may have been burgled, do not stop. Walk straight past and go to a neighbour; you can call the police from there. If you pull up outside your house and see evidence of a break-in, turn around and drive off. The criminal may be fooled into thinking you were just turning around, and it gives you the opportunity to call the police immediately. You want to avoid confronting a criminal in your home if at all possible; the police enjoy catching burglars at work and generally respond quickly to a criminal in a home if you give them the opportunity.

At your door, stand sideways on rather than with your back to the street. This will allow you to keep your peripheral vision on the street. Once inside, establish a routine for checking that your house is secure.

If you are returning to an empty house and are concerned that someone may be either observing you or following you, then the 'home in a minute' call is a useful ploy to put doubt into a criminal's mind. Remember, a criminal will always take the easy option. As you are approaching the house with keys in hand, simply grab your phone and say loudly enough for whoever it is you are concerned about to hear: 'Hi Tom. Get the kettle on. I'll be a minute.' Another favourite is: 'Wake up, grumpy. It's me coming home, so don't let the dog out.' I'm sure you can come up with your own lines; the important thing is to make it short, sharp and believable. In reverse, if you are leaving the house and are concerned that you may be 'telegraphing' that your home is empty, then either shout 'goodbye' and 'sleep tight' as you leave, or wave to an imaginary person as you go. You will feel silly doing it, but if you create doubt in the mind of a criminal, you will have achieved the aim.

If you are going to use a taxi service to leave or return to your home, then there are a number of specific considerations. If you are able to, use the same company and always keep its number in your

PREVENT

phone. If you are away from home or new to an area, always use a recognised taxi company that you have to book, rather than minicabs touting for business. When you make the call, try to do it where you cannot be overheard. With a booked taxi, confirm with the driver who he is booked for, rather than offering your name first before you get in. If you do use a minicab, agree the price before you get in. Most disagreements arise from mis-

understandings about payment. If you are travelling alone, perhaps in an unlicensed taxi, consider using your camera phone to take an image of the driver and the car registration number, and text both to a friend, politely explaining to the driver that your partner insists on this.

If you're using a taxi on your own, consider using your camera phone to text an image of the driver to a friend.

If you are on your own in a taxi, sit directly behind the driver and keep conversation to a polite minimum. If at any point you become unhappy or uncomfortable, ask to be let out at a well-lit public place or fuel station. Once again, you can use the 'home in a minute' call as you approach your home. Finally, do not get dropped off outside your house, particularly if you are a single woman. It is better to get dropped about 100 metres away. This not only means the driver will not see where you live, but also allows you to go through your returning home routine and observe how your house looks before you enter.

When being collected from your house by taxi, always use a reputable company, as the driver will see if you are leaving an empty house for the evening. In addition to leaving lights, a TV or a radio on, the false 'wave goodbye' is a useful technique to put doubt into the mind of the driver.

We will look in detail at two types of vehicle crime: theft of a car and theft from a car. Carjacking has already been discussed in Chapter 2.

Theft of a car

The more you can do to protect your vehicle the better. But most importantly, don't leave it where criminals are likely to operate.

Modern car security systems are increasingly effective against all but the most professional thief, so if you have an alarm or immobiliser, use it. The addition of tracking products with clear labelling is also a good deterrent, as is a high-visibility steering or handbrake lock. All these things are common sense. If you want specific advice regarding car alarms or security systems, the list of Websites and Sources of Further Information includes details for Thatcham, which tests car alarms for security companies, and for approved car security system fitters.

PREVENT

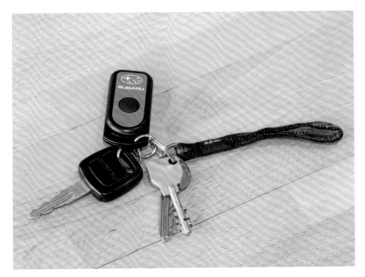

It's almost always easier to steal your keys than to break into your car.

More important than the car systems is the location you park your car. If you have a garage, use it. Not only will it mean your car is more secure; it will also keep it warm and dry, reducing maintenance costs, and your insurance company will lower your premium. If you don't have a garage, but have off-road parking, consider installing a folding pillar in your driveway to prevent your vehicle being stolen. This is the folding type of bollard that you can fix in the up position once you have driven over it. If you have to park on a street, avoid spots next to alleyways or other suitable escape routes for criminals and also locations where your car might get damaged – for example, outside a pub or by playing fields. If your car is stolen, report it immediately, along with any contents. The recovery figures for the UK are actually quite good.

Finally, be aware that criminals will try to target your keys. Treat your car keys as a valuable item. At home, keep all your keys in one spot. The best solution is a small securable cabinet; many burglaries are actually committed to get car keys. If you are at work or out and about, keep your keys with you and hidden from view, particularly if you drive a valuable car with a distinctive key fob.

The simplest way to ensure the contents are not stolen with the car is to keep nothing of value in the vehicle when it is parked. The only things that should remain in it permanently should be items you can replace and that have no sentimental value – for example, your safety box in the boot.

Theft from a car

Once again, the location of your car is crucial. Try to leave it in well-lit and visible areas and avoid locations with good escape routes such as alleyways or entrances to playing fields. Remember, car crime doesn't only happen in built-up areas. Groups of car thieves operate in rural beauty spots, targeting vehicles left by people taking walks, so always ensure you leave your vehicle in a safe condition.

Leaving your valuables on show in your car is asking for trouble.

There is a simple way to decide what to leave in your car. Imagine the windows are stuck in the down position. If you wouldn't be happy to leave something in the main body of your car with the windows down, then it shouldn't be there. Thieves will take no notice of windows; they offer no security.

If you find you have to leave something in your car while it is unattended, try to put it into the boot. This includes your stereo or removable satellite navigation system. If this is not possible, you need to get the desirable object out of sight as much as possible. Move items under the seat or into the footwell. If you are stuck with a bag or other potentially attractive item, consider using your car blanket to cover it over.

PREVENT

An Englishman's home is always said to be his castle. Unfortunately, the truth in the UK today is a little different. In three out of ten burglaries in 2006 no force was required to enter; the criminal got in through an open door or window. About a third of burglars entered through windows

and two-thirds through doors. From these simple facts we can deduce that, if doors and windows are relatively secure, the risk of burglary is significantly reduced. In addition to this, 60 per cent of burglaries against homes with alarms were unsuccessful. Below you will find some very basic advice on home security. More detailed guidance is available from contacts in the list of Websites and Sources of Further Information. When considering home security, think like a burglar and ask yourself: 'How would I get in if I lost my keys?'

Don't invite burglars into your home – keep your doors and windows closed.

Location, location, location

The first step in considering all the factors that affect your home's security is to look at where you are located. Homes at the end of terraces are more likely to be burgled than those in the centre. Lone houses on the outskirts of urban areas are vulnerable, as are homes with gardens that back onto alleyways or waste land. Get outside, have a walk round and look for what the criminal looks for: a route in and a route out. Can you get to your house without being seen by using an alleyway or crossing a park? If so, you need to protect your home specifically from these approaches. If you are

Be confident about your front door – the lock, some kind of alarm and a fire extinguisher

Houses with alarms are less likely to be burgled

A low light constantly on around your front door discourages burglars and doesn't annoy your

Keep clutter to a minimum around the main entrance to your home to prevent someone hiding **(4)**

Feel safe in your master bedroom; ensure you can call 999 from your bed and consider fitting locks and a panic alarm **(5)**

Most burglaries are made though open doors or windows; keep your windows closed and locked **(6)**

Laying gravel under windows or around fences makes moving quietly impossible **(7)**

Use PIR sensor lights only in areas that need protecting and ensure they do not annoy your neighbours **(8)**

Think about what goes into your rubbish; shred or burn anything with bank or personal details **(9)**

Fitting 'flimsy' trellis to the top of walls and fences makes it impossible to climb quietly **(10)**

Planting 'angry' plants around your border will discourage trespassers **(11)**

Burglars love hidden approach routes to homes. If there is one near your house, protect yourself against it.

buying a new house, bear this in mind when you are viewing the sites. If the house is beautiful but backs onto derelict buildings or waste land, consider reducing your offer to take into account any security work you think may be necessary.

Doors and windows

Impartial advice on the best door and window security measures for your home can be gained from your local police crime reduction officer. In the UK the Master Locksmiths Association works with British Standards to lay down the guidelines that people like insurance companies and property developers will consider as a base level. Details of both websites can be found in the list of Websites and Sources of Further Information. BS 8220-1 is the 'Guide for Security of Buildings against Crime'; Part 1 covers 'Dwellings'. The Master Locksmiths Association produces a useful document called the 'Guidelines for Minimum Security Requirements for Domestic Property', which can be downloaded for free from its website.

When considering your doors and windows, remember that, while some insurance companies may accept security measures that don't conform to the British Standards, the BS marks are a useful guide for the average person. I would advise buying security furniture that conforms to or exceeds British Standards. For an in-depth survey you should contact a professional, but the advice given below indicates the basic level of security you should have on doors and windows in your home. It's not the most exciting subject in the world, but get it wrong and you might not only lose your belongings, but also find that your insurance company won't cover the loss.

Your front door doesn't necessarily need to be new to be secure. Ensure you have the right locks and chain fitted.

Front doors

Your external door furniture should conform to BS 3621, and if the door is to be used as a fire exit and you need to be able to use the door without a key, ensure it conforms to BS 8621. Your locksmith or DIY centre will be able to provide detailed advice. An external door should be fitted with a primary 'latch'-type lock that conforms to either BS 3621 or BS 8621 as an absolute minimum; however, it is sensible to consider the following additional measures.

Additional mortice deadlock. This is an additional lock that should sit midway between the standard lock and the top or bottom of the door, depending on which is the greatest distance away. This is not a 'latch' type but a deadlock.

Additional mortice or rim security bolts. These bolts fit either horizontally or vertically onto the opening side of the door. Horizontally, they fit midway between the existing locks and the top and bottom of the door; vertically they should be fitted between 50 and 100mm away from the edge of the door. For doors that need to be used as a fire escape, these bolts should be knob operated

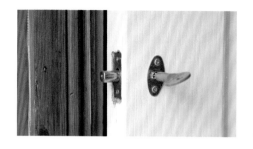

rather than key operated. It is also worth remembering that these bolts can be set only from inside and should not be locked if someone is still expected home. This type of lock is extremely useful in your 'safe room', which we will discuss later.

A mortice bolt can provide exrtra security.

Hinge bolts. These should be fitted to all outward-opening doors, because criminals can attack hinges. They are permanent studs fitted along the hinge side of the door that prevent such activity. Some hinges come with hinge bolts already fitted, so look and see what you have.

Letter box. Finally, consider where your letter box is. It shouldn't be fitted less than 400mm away from any locks, and you might consider installing a box to prevent anyone trying to reach in and grab anything. If exit through your door is 'keyless' and can be achieved by turning knobs, then you should not have a letter box. Instead fit a mail box outside your home.

Configuration. The best possible arrangement for your front entrance is a double door with a partially glazed exterior door that can be opened quickly and a secure internal door fitted with the security measures described above. This has three advantages. First, on returning to your home, you can gain access quickly to an area of relative safety by using one key. Secondly, when answering the door, you can maintain a physical gap between you and a caller. Finally, anyone attempting to break into your home will not only have to get through two doors, but will also be visible to passers-by while trying to defeat your main door locks.

If you do not want to go to the trouble of fitting a double entrance door, you can still enhance your safety by improving the security of the approach to your front door and fitting a front gate. Anything that puts a physical barrier between your property

PREVENT

and the public footpath is ideal. Not only does it slow down someone coming onto your property; it also ensures the criminal has to display intent. Imagine you live in an end terrace and have a small grass front garden with no fence. People may walk over your garden to cut the corner; it is difficult to tell whether anyone on your lawn is cutting the corner or looking in your windows. Install a fence around your garden, and someone standing in your garden when you return home clearly has intent to do something.

Finally, clear any clutter around your front door that anyone could hide behind. You should be able to see the area of your front door as you approach from any direction, so ensure it is lit at night-time.

Other entrances

There is little point having Fort Knox as your front entrance and an internal door with a sliding bolt as a back door. Ensure that all your doors can be adequately secured to prevent easy access. Particularly consider any entrances that are covered from view. This might include external garage doors or utility room exits.

In much the same way that you should carefully consider the location of your letter box, make sure that your cat or dog flap is not positioned within easy reach of your door lock, bolt or handle. Larger dog flaps should be secured when you are not at home. You would be amazed at the small space needed for human access to a house.

Take advice on securing other types of doors you may have. Modern sliding patio doors normally come fitted with anti-lift locks, but many older types do not have them. It is also worth considering the glazing in your doors and whether it could benefit from being improved. Replacing with laminated glass or fitting double glazing with security film can be very effective in preventing entry.

Check whether your patio doors are fitted with anti-lift locks.

Answering the door

Establish a routine for opening your door and ensure everyone in your home uses it. Take time with your children to teach them how to answer the door and reinforce the message by sticking to the system yourself.

The correct system is shown below:

1. *Decide whether to answer the door at all. If you're not expecting anyone, there is no reason to go to the door. This may sound rude, but a sensible solution is to have a cut-off time. Deciding not to answer the door after 7 p.m. is a useful start point.*

2. *If in doubt, view the door from the first floor. Particularly if you are elderly or feel vulnerable, this is a great way to identify who is calling. Open the first-floor window nearest to your front door and ask what the caller wants. Your door remains closed and you have a good distance between you and the caller. Most unwanted callers can be dealt with from here with a 'No thank you'.*

3. *At the door, look first using your window or spy hole to confirm who is there.*

4. *Put the chain or bar on before you open the door.*

Always answer the door with the chain on.

5. Confirm the identity of the person calling. Don't just glance at his or her ID. Take it and inspect the front and the back. If you want to confirm the person's identity, take the card and call the company. Close your door when you do this. If you're not happy, then ask the person to make an appointment and come back. Most companies that make home calls now operate a password system that is agreed before a home visit. Ask the company arranging a visit if they operate a password system.

6. Before you open your door and let someone into your home, particularly if you are on your own, think 'Are you sure?' If not, ask the person to come back when someone else is with you.

7. When people you do not know come to your house, limit their visits to the parts of the building they need to see and do not leave them unattended at any point. Finally, make sure that a visitor has not left anything in your home, particularly near computers or your alarm system.

Finally, you may decide it is sensible to ensure the area near your door is balanced in your favour. Consider fitting a permanent panic alarm near the door, or a hand-held panic alarm on a wall mount. You may also wish to think about what is 'to hand' near your door, and add something to deter a possible intruder, like a CO_2 fire extinguisher or some other item with which to protect yourself.

Before you open your door completely, think 'Am I sure?' It is too late to change your mind once it's open.

Windows

Anyone who really wants to gain entry to your home (or car for that matter) will smash a window. If you believe that a criminal would have the motivation to do this, then consider three courses of action. First, windows that are not required as fire exits can be fitted with decorative bars. This is becoming more common and in many countries is the norm. Secondly, you could upgrade your glazing by using a security film or even by fitting laminated or toughened glass; this of course will not be cheap. Finally, you can fit an alarm and internal security measures to prevent the criminal from gaining access to your valuables. In most instances, burglars will try to avoid smashing a window if they can simply gain access through an open window or door.

If not required as a fire exit, windows can be covered with decorative bars.

Windows that are not required to be opened should be screwed shut. Windows that need to be opened infrequently should be fitted with a device that will secure them in the open or closed position and that is operated by some form of key. That way, the criminal needs to smash a hole large enough to gain access rather than make a small hole and then undo the latch.

Windows that are required as fire exits should be fitted with latches that are knob operated for ease of use. However, to prevent someone smashing a small area and undoing the window, you should consider installing laminated glass or film protection on these windows.

All glass should be in accordance with BS 6262 or BS5357 for security-enhanced glazing.

Remember, if a burglar really wants to gain access to your home, he will probably be able to, in the same way that, if you lock your house and then lose the keys, you could probably get in eventually with the help of your neighbour's tool kit and a ladder. Your aim is to deter the oppor-

PREVENT

There are many different types of window fastener. If possible ensure your locks conform to BS standards.

tunist thief and make life as hard as possible for the determined burglar. You can do this by slowing his progress to the point where he will not be able to find or gain access to your valuables before someone is alerted to his presence. An alarm is the best way of doing this, and we will consider this later.

Is your home attractive to burglars?

Imagine for a moment that you are a burglar. How would you conduct your business? You are looking for houses that are easy to get into, houses that you know will be vacant or homes that you know have items of significant value. You will probably invest considerable time looking for property that fits any one of these criteria or if possible all three. Now consider your own home and whether it fits any of the three criteria? Do you advertise that your security is poor by leaving windows open during the day time, or is your front door old and ill fitting? Do you leave your house with all the lights off and no sign of occupation? Is it possible to see your brand new TV and DVD player from the street? Aim to advertise as little as possible. If at a quick glance the profile of your home is that of a secure and occupied house with little immediately worth stealing, then the criminal will take an easier option.

Advertising issues to consider in detail are:

Does your house look secure? Wrought-iron grilles are increasingly being installed on windows that are not required as fire exits. They provide both actual security and a very visual impression of a secure building. We will discuss alarms later, but an illuminated alarm box on the front of your home is a fantastic deterrent; in a recent poll of known burglars, over 90 per cent had alarms fitted to their own homes! A useful lesson. Ensure your windows are closed before you leave and that they are obviously secured with fixings. Leaving the brass fixtures of your locks apparent demonstrates that they are in use.

An alarm box can act as a deterrent to the casual observer.

PREVENT

Does your house look empty when you leave? Are there any lights on in your home and do they switch on and off while you are out? Is there a TV or radio on in the house? These things are very easy and cheap to achieve with a visit to your DIY shop and the purchase of plug-timer switches. When you go away on holiday, cancel your papers and milk delivery. Ensure you get someone to visit the house every few days to clear your mail and if possible to spend a few hours there, either watching TV or having a meal. You will probably find someone who is very happy to use your facilities for free; it will ensure your home appears occupied while you are away, and that it remains in good working order.

Timer switches are a cheap and practical way to make your home appear occupied.

Is it possible to spot attractive items from outside your home? Many people despise net curtains, but they do reduce the possibility of seeing your valuables from the street. Other options include blinds or film on the downstairs windows that face public areas. There are some very good films on the market that offer either a tint or frosting at very reasonable prices. The bonus is that these films all offer at least some extra strength to your glazing. If for some reason you really want people to be able to look into your home, then at least ensure that in the rooms visible from the street no highly attractive items are on show. Also consider what other things signal that there are valuable items in your home. Do not leave boxes for brand new TVs or electrical items outside your house; crush them down and put them in a bin bag before you place them outside.

Are you careful with your rubbish?

Your rubbish says a lot about you and anyone taking a genuine interest in you or your home will certainly have a good look in your bin in the process of deciding whether to commit a crime against you. If you are affluent and lucky enough to buy expensive items on a reasonably regular basis, you will at some point throw away the receipts. Finding a receipt in your rubbish for jewellery or an expensive laptop will certainly encourage a criminal to carry out further investigation.

Your rubbish identifies you. For a number of reasons, you should think carefully about how to manage your household waste.

Identity theft

Beyond the information that can be gained from your rubbish, there is the more pressing concern of identity theft. While this is not a violent crime, I have included it because it is part of your overall security to ensure you protect your identity. Never dispose of letters concerning any of your financial information in your general refuse. If you still do this, then change your habit immediately. Identity theft is one of the fastest growing crimes in the UK, and we all need to get much better at preventing it. An easy way to deal with the problem is to take on the system used by offices that deal with classified information: have a general waste bin and a 'burn bag'.

Anything with your bank or personal details on it goes in the burn bag. Once your burn bag is full, either shred it using a home shredder or have a weekly, monthly or quarterly burn. Home shredders need not be expensive and you can buy something suitable for most homes for about £50, a small price to pay compared with the losses resulting from identity theft, which cost each adult in the UK an average of £35 in 2005. Ensure you also collect receipts when you are out and about. If you are poor at keeping track of receipts, set aside a particular car door pocket or similar receptacle for paperwork, and empty it regularly into your burn bag at home. You should also shred or burn anything that clearly identifies when your home will be empty – for example, details about your forthcoming holiday. Unfortunately, the more you think about it, the more mail you will want to put in the burn bag, so perhaps it is worth investing in a shredder rather than polluting the environment with all that smoke!

Household shredders are relatively inexpensive and can give you peace of mind.

Alarm systems

Quite simply, you get what you pay for. Fitting something cheap from a DIY store will have little effect on a determined burglar and may be a waste of money.

It is possible to be bamboozled by science and the superior capability of one system over another once you invite an alarm system salesman to your home, so before you spend hundreds if not thousands of pounds, consider two things. Will you use the alarm, and will it pass the walk-by test.

Most people I know with very expensive alarm systems never set them because it takes too long or is too inconvenient. If this is likely to be you, then there is little to be gained from spending lots of money. The best people to speak to really are the experts, but ensure that whatever you decide to have fitted complies with the British and European standards. If you are confused and want impartial advice, your local police crime reduction officer will be able to help and is a good startpoint.

Also consider the walk-by test; once again imagine you are the burglar and think about the profile of your house. Burglars know what real systems look like. However, most alarm companies will fit real alarm boxes without the rest of the system at a greatly reduced price. If it passes the walk-by test, it's worth it.

The British Security Industry Association (BSIA) is the professional trade association for the security industry in the UK. Using a company that is a member of the BSIA will ensure it has met certain criteria in terms of professionalism and standards.

There are two main bodies that act as an inspectorate for companies that fit alarms. These are the NSI and the smaller SSAIB.

The NSI is a not-for-profit organisation that provides the NSI NACOSS Gold scheme and the NSI Silver scheme, which replaced the older ICON scheme.

The SSAIB is an independent inspectorate.

By using a company that is regulated by these bodies you will have a bench mark in terms of the service you should expect. The BSIA, NSI and SSAIB all have websites that provide useful information if you are thinking of fitting an alarm system and can provide lists of approved companies in your area.

When you decide to invite someone to quote for an alarm system, make sure the company is approved by one of these bodies and also ensure you approach more than one firm. Whoever you choose, you should check that the survey visit is free and that after the visit you will receive:

●   *a written risk assessment based on a full survey*

- *a full quote of costs, including the standards conformed to, that you can send to your insurer for approval*

- *written confirmation that after fitting you will receive full certification that the system is compliant with all British and European standards*

Almost all companies should be able to do this for you, and you should avoid those that will not. Companies that are not registered may not vet their employees, or you may find that you have spent money on an alarm that your insurance company will not recognise.

In simple terms there are two types of alarm: the 'bells-only' system and the 'monitored' system.

The bells-only system is the simpler and cheaper option, and for everyday life in a busy household with children and perhaps pets it is probably the answer. It can provide perimeter protection, and can be easily set and disarmed. This means that doors and windows can be protected. But this system is not connected to a central control room. It will alert you to an intruder, and may frighten an intruder away in your absence. But police will respond to the alarm only if someone calls them to report suspicious activity or a break-in.

Whatever type of alarm you decide on, ensure it is fitted by a reputable company.

A monitored alarm is much more expensive. It is connected to a central control room, which is manned round the clock. The system achieves a 'confirmed' signal by having at least two sensors covering places where a criminal may enter, so sensors have to be fitted inside the house, and the number of sensors needed will increase the overall cost. This type of system also incurs an annual service fee. There are specific requirements to be fulfilled before the control room is able to call a family member or the police.

A happy compromise if you do want to be safe in the knowledge that someone has called the police is a panic alarm. Unlike a full alarm system, this does not need to be set and can be left always 'armed'. In most cases, if a panic alarm is activated, the control centre will immediately call the police. Many people, and particularly the elderly or those at risk, are less worried about knowing their home is safe when they are absent than they are about knowing they can get attention if someone is in their home, or they need help. Panic alarms should be fitted in your master bedroom and possibly by your front door, but ensure they are well covered to prevent accidental activation. Wireless panic alarms can also be used and kept around the neck.

Finally, remember that if you have no budget you can always try bluff. While you're not going to fool the seasoned professional, if you install a dummy alarm box and a convincing 'alarm-fitted' sign, you might put doubt into the mind of the apprentice criminal.

Access control and CCTV

Access control is particularly useful for people who are at risk.

If you have the budget, and your own threat assessment indicates that you may need to improve your security beyond that afforded by a secure building and a decent alarm system, then other

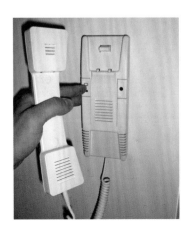

CCTV is a great deterrent and is becoming more affordable.

PREVENT

technology is available. Access control systems are particularly useful for anyone who wants to confirm the identity of callers and specifically can be beneficial for those who may be 'at risk' – for example, the elderly. CCTV is a fantastic deterrent and either overt or covert systems can provide evidence of criminal activity to assist in prosecution. If you are interested in additional security measures, it is best to take specialist advice, either from your local police crime reduction officer or from a security equipment provider.

Plants, gravel and lights

You can discourage people from even getting near to your house by using plants, gravel and lights around the perimeter of your property. Consider growing thorny plants to discourage entry. Ensure they are not so high as to provide cover but high enough to mean an uncomfortable crossing. A boundary can also be improved by trellis on a solid wall. Walls and solid fences are easy to climb. Topping your boundary with a flimsy trellis or fence makes it very difficult to climb. The addition of an unpleasant plant makes an outstanding natural barrier.

In your garden, ensure that solid structures such as sheds or gazebos are not close enough to your building to act as an improvised ladder and can't be moved for the same reason.

Criminals hate gravel; it is noisy and stops them from being able to creep about. A particularly effective idea is to create a gravel 'moat' around your house. This not only discourages people from lurking around your windows, but also acts as fantastic natural drainage around your walls. Similarly, if there is an approach to your home that you are concerned about, consider putting down gravel, with cactus or similarly unpleasant plants as a barrier.

Gravel is easy to maintain and can act as a good deterrent.

Exterior lighting should be carefully considered. Lights with sensors that turn them on and off can be annoying for you and your neighbours and can also be dangerous for passing traffic. Far better for most areas are night lights that provide a constant low level of illumination. Protecting the approach to your front and rear doors with a sensor light is sensible, but ensure you fully consider the effect of it coming on and off before you spend money.

Finally on lighting, ensure that the area around your front door is lit. The best solution is a double entrance with internal lighting. If you don't have a double entrance, then use a low-watt exterior light fitted well out of reach.

Dogs and other deterrents

A dog is one of the best deterrents against burglary.

Once again step into the mind of the burglar and consider what might be on the inside of a house that would put you off? Certainly a dog or indication that a dog may be present would be a deterrent. You can buy a 'beware of the dog' sign for your front door for less than £5. If it creates doubt in the criminal's mind, he will go

elsewhere. If you are genuinely worried about your security, then a loyal dog is just about the best thing you can have. Owning a dog is a huge commitment, and one that carries with it responsibility as well as enormous rewards. You will find details about the Kennel Club, which can offer advice about owning a dog, in the list of Websites and Sources of Further Information.

Other deterrents include the occupants of the home or regular visitors to it. If you live near a friend or member of the family who is elderly or at risk, there are many reasons why a frequent visit is a good-spirited action. The opportunist thief can strike at any point, but career criminals will plan their actions. Knowing that a potentially easy victim has regular visitors could create enough doubt to send the criminal elsewhere.

PREVENT

Safes

Home safes are now very reasonably priced and you can find something suitable for the average house for around £60. Of course you will need to spend more for a quality item, but securing your best jewellery and key documents like passports and birth certificates in a safe will protect them from the average house burglar. The most sensible place to fit a safe is where you will use it, not necessarily where it is most secure. There are plenty of expensive floor safes in hidden-away cupboards that are completely empty because they are inconvenient to use. Fitting a simple safe on one of the shelves in your master bedroom provides usable security for your jewellery and key documents. Remember, though, that burglars tend to target the master bedroom in a house first, and also the living area. Children's rooms, interestingly, are hardly ever looked at. If you have a home office or area where your PC and personal data are kept, consider fitting a simple safe next to the PC and putting the hard drive away at night.

A simple padlock with a clasp and staple fitting is a cheap but effective deterrent for an endless list of household situations.

Locking your valuable items away can also defeat the casual or opportunist thief. Simple clasp and staple fittings with padlocks are a very good idea for garage cupboards or storage containing tools or valuable items. If you're going on holiday, consider locking internal doors. Students leaving their digs for the long summer break should consider

spending a little money on securing their valuables before heading off. Student accommodation holds notoriously good pickings for burglars during the summer.

If you have a shed or outbuilding, ensure that the items within it are locked away securely. A simple way to do this is to use a chain and padlock to weave between items like lawn mowers and leaf blowers. Keep locks on the drawers or cupboards containing your tools.

Safe rooms

We think long and hard about how to secure our belongings, but rarely consider how we would secure ourselves, except for locking our front door. The properly designed and fitted safe room is something that only the very wealthy can afford; it is, however, easy to achieve the same effect on a very small budget.

You will use a safe room only if you believe someone is in your home. At this point you will want to do two things: contact the police and prevent the intruder getting to you until they arrive. It is most likely that you will be worried about an intruder at night-time, so the sensible option is to have your safe room near your master bedroom.

If you have a landline telephone in your master bedroom and you take your mobile phone to bed, then the logical solution is to turn your master bedroom into the family safe room. Ensure the phone will work in case of a power cut. If you also have a panic alarm fitted next to your bed, then you have three methods of communicating with the outside world. Whichever room you choose, you need to ensure you can protect the door and that easy access cannot be gained to the windows. In most cases fitting a solid fire door with mortice bolts at the top and bottom and hinge bolts is good enough to keep someone out for long enough for the police to arrive. Such a door and fittings can be bought for just over £100, and are sound investments.

Fitting mortice bolts to a fire door on your master bedroom means you have a safe haven in your home.

Dealing with an intruder

The worst possible event imaginable for many people is finding an intruder in their home. There are three potential scenarios: coming home to find a burglar already in your house; a break-in during the day when you are at home; and a break-in at night-time. In all

Confronting an intruder in your home at night is a scenario most of us fear. Make a plan now as to how you will deal the situation.

situations, the best possible outcome is for you to avoid the intruder and call the police.

Arriving home to find an intruder will come as a surprise! Do not expect to be able to deal with the situation with a level head; your instincts will take over. The first way to reduce the risk of the situation occurring is to ensure that you get into the routine of observing your home on approach. Remember, if you see something suspicious, do not enter your house; call the police from a neighbour's home. The next key routine is a quick check of your home every time you return. This need not be some paranoid activity you conduct with a fire poker in hand. Think of it more as a safety check for leaks and electrical problems. Once you get used to doing this, it provides a real sense of normality and safety when you get home.

If at any time you are in your home and become aware of an intruder in another room, the safest course of action is to leave and call the police. If this is not possible – for example, if the intruder is between you and your exit – first call the police and then either hide or, if that is not possible, try to create a barrier between you and the intruder. In either circumstance, if there is a room or barrier between you and the intruder, use it to your advantage and call for help. If you have a safe room in the house, then head for it if you can. In secure residences I have worked in, there has been a more secure room on each floor, so that wherever you are you have somewhere to go. If you are genuinely concerned about the possibility of an intruder, consider fitting mortice and hinge bolts to one of your downstairs rooms.

If you stumble into one another, then how things proceed will, to a certain extent, depend upon your instincts. Unless you have been given formal training, then your instinctive reaction will be 'fright', 'fight' or 'flight'. It is very difficult to predict how you will react. As an example, I have an acquaintance who had his children with him when an intruder appeared on his property. Afterwards he could logically reason that the most sensible course of action would have been to scare the intruder off and remain close to his family. However, his fight instinct, fuelled by his outrage, was so strong that he found himself chasing the criminal for some distance before the mist cleared and he became aware of his actions. He described his overwhelming desire to fight to protect his family, even though he had no idea about whether the criminal was armed or in any way dangerous. The best advice, always, is not to get involved, but you need to accept that you will not be logical if this kind of event happens to you.

Unless you have been trained otherwise, whatever your instinct is, go with it and amplify it. The worst case is that you naturally 'fright' and become stationary with fear. Thinking about such an incident before it happens and having a plan can ensure that you 'flight' or 'fight', so consider how you might react. If you do find yourself frozen with fear, it is imperative that you try to override your natural instinct and do something. Use the fear energy to run if you can.

If your natural instinct is flight, then amplify this by screaming and bolting for your nearest exit point. Use the increased energy and strength you will have from the huge shot of adrenalin triggered by encountering the intruder, and do not stop screaming until you are outside. Once outside, get attention by shouting and calling for assistance.

If your instinct is to fight, sensible advice not to become engaged with the intruder is likely to have little effect. Moreover, if you have your children with you or someone you feel you should protect, there is every chance that all the advice in the world will not stop you from fighting to protect your family group. Once again, if you really can't help yourself, go with your instinct and amplify it. You will have the advantage of adrenalin, outrage and surprise; make sure you use it. You will

Criminals don't only operate at night-time; have a plan to deal with daytime intruders too.

find guidance in Chapter 8 about how to ensure someone no longer poses a threat, but remember you can legally pick up anything to hand to protect yourself, and you can keep acting until you believe the intruder no longer poses a threat to your safety.

A break-in during the day when you are already at home can be treated in the same way as coming home to find an intruder: call the police, keep a physical barrier between you and the intruder if possible, and head for a safe room if you have one. If you come face to face, go with your instinct and amplify it. If you are frozen with fear then try to turn this into flight. If your instinct is to run, then be noisy and focused. If despite all the best advice you decide to fight, then don't stop until the threat has passed.

During the day, there are many possible scenarios of where you and the intruder may be, hence you have to rely to a certain extent on your instincts and make a decision in the heat of the moment. The night-time intruder scenario is more of a set-piece battle and there is much you can do beforehand to tip the scales in your favour. You have all had the nightmare or considered the situation. You're in bed when you hear the unmistakable noise of someone downstairs. What do you do? The simple guide below should help (the guide is based on a family unit of Dad, Mum and two children). This plan is not the be all and end all, but it is a plan. Deciding to do something and going with it is invariably better than deciding to do nothing. Whatever your personal circumstances, ensuring you have thought about this situation will enable you to sleep feeling safer.

Tip the scales in your favour by being able to call 999 from your bed.

You are sure someone is in your home and you have a master bedroom safe room:

1. **Call for assistance.** *If you are sure that someone is in your home, there is little point creeping down the stairs carrying a rolled-up newspaper. Call for assistance immediately by dialling 999 or activating your panic alarm.*

2. **Move the family to a place of safety.** *(Some advice states that by making a noise you may scare off an intruder; my opinion is that, if you are going to make a noise anyway, make it doing something useful.) The strongest member of the family (normally Dad) takes station at the top of the stairs with something to use as a weapon, while someone else (Mum) collects the*

children and tells them to go to the master bedroom. You all move into the master bedroom and lock the bolts you have fitted on your solid door and await the imminent arrival of the police.

2a.   **If you have no safe room upstairs.** *Mum hides with the children in a pre-thought-of spot and Dad draws a mental line between the intruder and the family. This is the line that you will not let anyone pass. The top of the stairs is a good spot in most houses. He waits there with some kind of weapon that is to hand, and, should the intruder cross that line, he acts with surprise and aggression to disable the intruder immediately. If someone is in your home, you do not have to wait to be attacked before attacking him.*

You hear a noise downstairs that may be the cat but that needs to be investigated:

1.   **Move the family to a place of safety.** *It is not sensible to have Dad wandering around downstairs with a rolled-up newspaper while the rest of the family is still asleep. If for no other reason than to practise the plan and turn it into a game for the children, it is always sensible to move your family to a place of safety if you are uncomfortable.*

A noise downstairs in the night may not be your cat.

2.   **Strongest member of the family investigates.** *(Dad earns his breakfast.) This is the time to switch all the lights on and make a noise to let the intruder know you are at home. Grab something to hand to use as a weapon and, once you see any evidence to suggest an intruder, return immediately to your place of safety and alert the police. Should Mum hear anything that indicates to her that Dad is in trouble, she calls the police immediately or pushes the panic alarm. She keeps the door locked.*

If you are on your own and are sure there is an intruder, lock yourself in and call the police. If you are not sure, you can either look or wait it out. If you decide to investigate, grab something to hand to use as a weapon and switch on all the lights. Before you leave your room, dial the numbers 999 into your phone but don't press call. Hold this in your non-dominant hand as you investigate your house. If you decide you really don't want to discover if it was the cat or an intruder, then of course you can simply lock the door to your bedroom and wait it out.

Finally, there is the worst possible scenario of waking to find someone already in your room. Again, you will react with your instincts rather than with logic, so you can tip the balance in your favour before it happens by ensuring that your bedroom is set up for you to look after yourself. It should not be possible for anyone

to creep into your room. This is particularly relevant if you are a student living in halls or somewhere where people can gain access directly to where you sleep. Sleeping in a locked room has implications in the event of a fire, but you need to decide what is best on balance. Sometimes you may be better to secure your room with a lock that can be opened quickly in an emergency. Fitting chimes to the back of your door or door handle provides you with the certainty that your door is still shut and no one is in your room. Anything that makes a noise is suitable, and the creaking door or floor board should be welcomed and not fixed.

Door chimes can alert you to an unwanted intruder.

In all situations you can defend yourself in your home with something to hand. Ensuring that there is something to hand in the right places in your home is not against the law. So keeping your golf clubs in the cupboard at the top of the stairs and a walking stick by your bed is sensible storage. Advice on the law and protecting yourself in your home can be found on the Home Office website, the details of which are in the list of Websites and Sources of Further Information.

PREVENT

In all the cases we have discussed there is a fine legal line between defending yourself and malicious violence. There is nothing to be gained from attacking someone already on the ground whom you have incapacitated, and attacking someone who has already left your property and who poses no threat is also against the law. However, if it really comes to the crunch and you believe you are acting to defend your life or that of your family, the law will protect you.

Advice for the elderly or those at risk

Many criminals perceive the elderly or people who are either physically or mentally impaired as easy targets. If you are in any of these groups or are concerned for someone who is, then feel confident that sensible precautions will afford protection. In many cases people in these groups find it easier to demonstrate secure behaviour that others might feel self-conscious about – for example, refusing to answer a door, or openly carrying a panic alarm.

Criminals target those who are most vulnerable. If you are worried or someone you know might be targeted, consider what you can do to help.

Access control. If you are worried about answering the door, the best solution is simply not to do it. Those from at-risk groups should seriously consider refusing to answer the door unless they are expecting a visitor, or installing a low-cost intercom or access-control device. This ensures that a physical barrier remains between you and any unexpected visitor and also prevents you being drawn into conversation. Some confidence tricksters can be very persuasive, so denying them the opportunity even to start a conversation is the best course of action.

Access control for family or carers. Some people who live at home need to be able to provide access to a member of their family or carers without being physically able to answer the door. The best possible solution is to ensure that anyone who needs access to your home has a key. However, this is not always possible. Some caring organisations do not send the same person every day and ask to be let in or, worse, ask for a key to be left outside or with a neighbour. You should never leave a key outside your home. Criminals know where to look for these 'hidden' spots and will find them. If your caring organisation does send different people, ensure you check their identity each time they arrive.

Key safe. In the extreme, it may become necessary for people who don't already have a key to be able to gain access to your home. One possibility in this situation is to use a key safe. When fitting a key safe, ensure it is placed in a location that is out of sight from the street. Also ensure that the combination to the box is given out only to those who need it and change it on a regular basis.

Shopping. If you still do your own shopping, then anything you can do to reduce the amount you have to carry is a great idea. Having your shopping delivered achieves a number of things; it reduces the amount of cash you need to carry around on your person; it means you don't need to spend time loading bags of

PREVENT

shopping into and out of your car; and it ensures that you can enjoy trips out of your home without worrying about unnecessary details. If you are not confident enough to arrange your own home shopping, ask someone to help you.

Personal alarm. If you feel that perhaps you are not as physically robust as you once were, then you can give yourself some self-confidence by carrying a personal alarm. When you're out and about, you should have a personal alarm to hand, and if you're really concerned, you can find alarms with a fob that goes around the wrist. With these, if someone tries to take it from your hand, it will automatically be set off. At home you may already have a help button that you carry, so you can gain attention if you have a fall or accident. This can be complemented by a monitored alarm system with a wireless panic button.

Wheelchair use. If you use a wheelchair, think about where you are going to keep your day kit. It has become routine for many people to hang a small bag on the back of the chair. This is not a great idea, because you can't see your belongings. Consider whether you can carry items on your lap or on the sides of your chair.

Keep your belongings to hand if you use a wheelchair and always carry a mobile phone and panic alarm.

Self-defence. If you are not physically robust, consider what you could carry to make you feel safe. Carrying a walking stick or umbrella could give you the short time you need to activate a personal alarm if necessary.

Advice for women

There are some specific concerns for women, largely relating to how to avoid or deter male predatory behaviour. By following the advice already given, you can reduce the risk significantly. To recap, do you:

- *feel confident that you are situationally aware when you are out and about? Would you notice if a man was following you?*

- *observe the people and space around you when you sit on public transport or in a public place?*

- *drive defensively, aware of the surroundings?*

- *feel confident with the security in your home?*

- *have a routine for getting into and out of your car and your home?*

- *have a plan for what you will do if you think someone is in your home?*

All these things are very simple. If you can confidently answer yes to each question, you are already managing your personal security and thus reducing the risk. But if you cannot answer yes to all of them, then perhaps you should revisit some areas of personal security in your life.

PREVENT

On your own?

If you live on your own, go out on your own, or find yourself spending time on your own, try not to advertise your situation. This has more components than you might think initially. At the basic level, if you live on your own in a flat, think about whether your name plate should say Miss P. Jones or simply P. Jones. If you are getting mail addressed to Miss Smith, then ensure you collect it daily and shred anything that obviously identifies you as someone who might be on her own at home.

Try to avoid overt signals that you live on your own or are a single female.

Consider the profile of your home. Can you be seen when you shower, or when you dress in the morning, or in your nightclothes when you turn the lights off before you go to bed? For some reason, there are women who feel a certain playful desire to be 'seen' at some point during the day. While this is a fascinating phenomenon and very interesting for the neighbours, do think about whether you might attract the wrong kind of attention.

On a wider issue, consider the general profile of your home to the outside world. Try to avoid creating a frontage that implies female-only occupancy or could act as an attraction to the type of man whose attention you don't want. I would not for one moment suggest that you should not decorate your home absolutely as you see fit, but much in the same way that it is unwise to place your plasma TV in the front room without net curtains, so it is probably also not entirely sensible to combine hanging your sexiest underwear in the side alley and leaving your desktop on the dates-direct home page in your front room.

On a more subtle level, keep your cards close to your chest when engaging in conversation. If you are out on your own, do not admit you are alone if asked. Always reply that you are expecting a friend or friends to join you or that you are expected to meet someone soon. If you start to become involved in conversation with someone whom you find uncomfortable, you can always say something along the lines of 'I'm really sorry but I have to call my friends or they will start to worry about me'. This also allows you to leave if you feel you need to.

In your handbag

I would absolutely insist that any woman outside a secure location like home or work should always have a mobile phone and if possible a panic alarm. This should apply in all situations, including

going out for a run, visiting a night-club or popping out to see a friend. You should already be maintaining situational awareness to PRE-EMPT trouble. Carrying a mobile phone will give you many more options to PREVENT your involvement in trouble. You can call a friend, ring for a taxi, pretend to call someone at home or ultimately call the police.

Your handbag should always have a mobile phone and an easily accessible panic alarm.

There are, of course, always exceptions, but a relatively fair assumption is that most females are less well adapted to engaging in physical violence than men. In the UK it is against the law to carry pepper spray or a purpose-built weapon, so the best thing you can carry is a panic alarm. As we discussed earlier, you need to ensure that you keep an alarm in an accessible place; you will not have time to hunt for it at the bottom of your handbag if you ever need it.

PREVENT

Being followed

If you are on foot and think you may be being followed, the first thing to do is confirm or deny your fear. Remember fear comes from a lack of knowledge, so if you start to feel uncomfortable with someone's presence, confirm whether he is actually focused on you. Take the time to have a look at him and assess what you think. There are a number of ways of doing this. If you are walking down a street, then cross the road and, as you do so, use the green cross code to your advantage – stand at the road side and, as you go through your looking left and right, take a long and deliberate look at the person you are uncomfortable with. If you do feel you are being followed, then you may not want to return to your home if you know it is unoccupied. A simple plan is to head for a busy populated area, so head for the town centre or perhaps a local shop where you know the owner is always in. Once you are in an area where you feel safe, you can then enter a shop or place of safety, and if the person is still in the area, call the police.

If you fear you are being followed, confirm your fear while heading towards a place of safety.

Advice to discuss with children

The best thing you can do for your children is to encourage behaviour that is security-aware from the outset. Ensuring that your children know that they should keep their valuables secure, and that it is not acceptable for others to take things, will mean that in later life they do not identify themselves as victims. Here are some specific things you might consider talking about with your children.

Understanding security

Throughout the book you will find advice about sensible planning for high-stress events – for example, an intruder in your home, or a fire. Ensure you have discussed what you as a family will do in such a circumstance and make sure your children understand what the plans are. In some instances it may even be prudent to explain and practise some routines with your children – for example, what to do if they are on their own at home and someone is at the door.

Getting in touch

There is a deal that can be made between children and grown-ups that you should always let each other know where you are going and how you can be contacted. If you demonstrate role-model behaviour from the outset, you have more chance of your children keeping you informed of their actions. If you are leaving the house and giving the details of where you are going to the babysitter, make sure you also explain to your children where you are going and what the phone number is.

The level of mobile phone theft between teenagers is astonishing, so if you do give your child a mobile, make sure you discuss when it is OK to use it and the fact that it should be kept

PREVENT

If you discuss and demonstrate secure behaviour with children from an early age it becomes habit. This is particularly relevant for mobile phone and MP3 player use.

in a pocket at all times when it is not being used. A good tactic to encourage this is to give your children the least attractive or fashionable phone you can find; sometimes giving them your old phone achieves this. The less likely they are to take it out and show it off, the less likely they are to be mugged for it.

Boundaries and rules

Curfew times, the distance they can travel away from home and who they can or cannot associate with are issues that all parents will discuss with their children at some point. It is, of course, up to each individual parent to decide where to draw the line, but the secret is to ensure that whatever you decide is achievable. Rather than have strict rules that you anticipate being broken regularly with little consequence, you may be better to set slightly more liberal rules but establish that the consequences of breaking them are significant. Children are people, and in many cases, if you discuss what they feel is fair and treat them like 'grown-ups', they will react accordingly and do their bit to conform.

Bullying

If you suspect that your children are being bullied, the best thing to do is to ask them directly if there is a problem, while reassuring them that talking about it is the best course of action. There could be a number of potential warning signs, including a reluctance to walk to school, or even to attend school. Physical signs may include damaged uniform or injury. Finally, behaviour may change, leading to mood swings, depression or nightmares. Of course all these kinds of behaviour could also be signs of other problems, or could have absolutely normal explanations. It is therefore essential to engage and speak with your child.

Bullying can be a difficult problem to solve. Try to let your child feel involved in finding a solution.

PREVENT

Once you have a good idea of what is happening, speak calmly and in detail to your child's class teacher or head teacher and request that the bullying is addressed. Almost all schools have a formal anti-bullying policy and you can ask to read it at any point.

It can be very hard to get children to talk openly about problems, so it may be that you need to provide the tools for them to feel as though they are resolving the difficulty themselves. The bullying website is a great source of information for kids and parents, and details can be found in the list of Websites and Sources of Further Information.

You are probably the last person your children will want to talk to about drug use or alcohol abuse, so don't be overly concerned if they are silent on these subjects.

Drugs and alcohol

It can be tremendously difficult to deliver a sound and reasoned message to growing children when it comes to drugs. The fact that two of the most devastating drugs in existence are legal in the UK at 18 can understandably create problems in rationalising why it is not only illegal, but also morally wrong, to become involved in drug use or alcohol abuse. Your children will receive drugs and alcohol advice at school, but if they want to know more, you will probably not be their first point of call. 'Talk to FRANK' is a tremendous service provided by the government. It has a website and a telephone hotline on 0800 77 66 00. Finally, for parents, it is worth remembering that almost a third of the UK adult population admit that they have used drugs at some point in their lives, but that doesn't necessarily mean they use them now.

Online safety

The Internet is a fantastic resource for children to learn about the world and also to interact with people globally. Like everything, though, it has risks that can be kept to a minimum as long as you discuss some simple rules with your child:

- *Discuss and agree an amount of time that it is acceptable to be online each evening.*

- *Children should never divulge online information relating to their address, telephone number or the school they attend. That includes the same information relating to their friends. They should also not divulge any password information.*

PREVENT

- *Children should not send photos over the Internet unless you agree to it.*

- *Children should not meet anyone they have contacted on the Internet unless you agree to it and attend the meeting.*

- *Children should not reply to any messages that make them feel uncomfortable and should alert you immediately.*

Most Internet service providers will install a filter for your children's log-in, to prevent them being exposed to anything of an unsuitable nature. You should, however, be aware that many children are far more IT literate than their parents, so leaving a child in a closed room with an Internet connection is never a great idea. If you are going to allow this, then ensure you have access to the machine, so you can check which sites have been visited. A better option is to consider positioning the computer your children use in a communal area, where you can see what they are browsing.

CHAPTER FIVE

Western Terrorism

Most UK residents have lived through the Irish Troubles and are used to the threat of terrorism. Since the 1970s we have accepted that unattended baggage should be viewed with suspicion. Compare this with the absolute paranoia in some areas of North America following 9/11 and it becomes clear that the UK population already has a reasonably measured view of the real risks posed by terrorism.

Since 9/11 the rules seem to have changed and the threat is new. Many of us feel uncomfortable with the new threats because they don't seem to follow the old rules. The shocking 7/7 attacks in London raised public fear to a different level, and sensational media reporting and rolling news led to a fear disproportionate to the level of risk.

This chapter does not focus on any particular terrorist group. Nor does it seek to identify a terrorist set of 'rules'; they don't exist. It does, however, outline general features common to most Western terrorist activities; it is for you to use the information as you see fit. You will learn what it is possible for terrorists to achieve, what the authorities are likely to be doing if and when an incident happens, and what you can do before, during and after a terrorist attack.

In this section you will find information regarding the various kinds of attack that terrorist organisations can mount. All options are covered so you have an understanding of the full spectrum of possible terrorist activity.

In the movies, a golden fireball rises slowly into the air and people brush themselves off. The reality is more usually a blinding flash, followed by a highly destructive blast wave picking up everything in its path and throwing it at supersonic speeds.

Things that go bang

Most of us can attribute our understanding of explosives to Hollywood movies. We see a bomb with an electronic timer counting down attached to something the size of a lunch box. The camera pans out and we see a huge fireball that brings down a family home, sending the star diving over the camera but picking himself up and dusting himself down. I'm afraid it's not quite like that. Most explosions have very little, if any, visible fireball; the damage to property is done by an invisible blast wave. To bring down a family home you need about a car's worth of explosive, and the most likely result of standing 50 metres away from a small blast is not that you will be thrown in an elegant arc, but rather that you will be shredded by fragments travelling at supersonic speeds.

PREVENT

Explosives and explosive accessories

Two groups of items are required to make something go bang: explosives and explosive accessories. Explosives can be subdivided into military, commercial or home-made; these provide the power. The explosive accessories are the detonators and fuses needed to convert the push of a button, an electric current or the strike of a match into a bang. For obvious reasons, we will not go into detail about any of the component parts, but we will look at the generics to give you a basic understanding of how things work.

Explosives

Military explosives are the sports utility of the explosive world, designed to be light and easy to use; they can be deployed for almost any purpose. They normally have a very large 'bang for your buck', and so are highly sought after by terrorist groups. They come packaged in ready-to-use forms and are extremely stable. You can hit most military explosives with a hammer and even burn small amounts as a fuel to boil water without them detonating.

Commercial explosives come in all shapes and sizes.

Commercial explosives are used in many industries you may not have thought of. Beyond mining and quarrying, they are employed to clear avalanches, in firefighting, in aerospace applications and in some medical procedures – for example, to shatter kidney stones! Their effects can be very well predicted, and they are manufactured specifically for purpose; so quarrying explosives will look different from those used in an ejector seat. Because they are used in such high quantities in the quarrying industry, commercial explosives are generally thought of as being easier to get hold of than military ones.

Home-made explosives are manufactured by terrorist organisations when they cannot get their hands on either military or commercial material. They normally do not have the same power-to-weight ratio, which means large quantities need to be used to achieve the same effect as a small amount of manufactured explosive.

There is no single way of recognising an explosive, but many have a waxy or oily residue and a distinctive smell; this can be a smell of almonds or a 'chemical' odour.

Explosive accessories

In order to make explosives detonate you need to convert a flame or heat, an electrical impulse or some kind of mechanical action into a detonation. There are many ways of doing this, but burning a safety fuse and using an electric detonator are the most common. It is relatively easy to recognise explosive accessories. Detonators tend to be cylindrical and are normally metallic; all safety fuses and detonating cords tend to look a bit like coloured washing line.

Explosive effects

Whatever the type of explosive used, some generic effects are always achieved:

- **Blast.** *The shock wave that is formed by the explosive itself can do damage to structures. The blast wave can also damage people, but its effectiveness drops off rapidly with distance. You get blast from all explosions.*

- **Blast incendiary.** *By adding chemicals to the explosive you can achieve the effect we see in Hollywood of a large fireball. There are limited practical uses for blast incendiary devices.*

- **Blast fragmentation.** *By putting fragments of metal or other material around an explosive you achieve a spray of fast-moving fragments that can do significant damage to soft items.*

PREVENT

- **Shaped charge.** By employing a method of channelling the power of the explosive, it is possible to achieve a very specific cutting or drilling effect.

Usually, terrorist devices fall into the blast fragmentation category. If they do not, it is normal that items immediately around the explosion will become 'secondary fragmentation', meaning that, in most instances, an explosive terrorist bomb will have both blast and fragmentation. Unless you are in the immediate vicinity of the explosion, the greatest threat to you is from fragmentation.

Types of explosive devices

Something manufactured in a factory for military purposes is normally referred to as explosive ordnance. Something made in a shed by a terrorist is normally referred to as an improvised explosive device or IED. There are many different types of IED, and they are normally described by how they are delivered and how they are initiated. So you may have a vehicle-borne (delivery) timer (initiation) device. In terms of initiation, the ways of making a bomb function are limited only by the bomb maker's imagination. You do not need to understand how a bomb works, but you may wish to think about how a terrorist might transport or place one.

Explosive ordnance has been manufactured by heavy industry normally for military purposes.

Put yourself into the mind of a terrorist and consider the delivery of your device. In simple terms you have two options: either to make it small enough to carry without drawing attention to yourself, or to put it in a vehicle, in which case you may as well make it as big as possible.

The largest item a person can carry without arousing suspicion is a rucksack or a holdall. It is likely that a device of this size will have a limited effect on solid structures like brick or concrete

An improvised explosive device has been manufactured in a terrorist bomb factory.

A holdall is about the largest item a person can carry easily without arousing suspicion. The relatively small amount of explosives that will fit in such a bag has a limited effect.

walls, unless it is placed immediately next to them. It is only in instances where the explosion causes a significant structural failure that large numbers of casualties occur – examples include the attack on the Grand Hotel in Brighton and the Oklahoma bomb. Because of this, a carried device will normally be designed to attack people and as such is likely to contain fragmentation. To protect ourselves from a device that is carried by someone, we need to get something solid between us and the device to shield us from the fragmentation. The effects of the blast will be worse in a confined space, but will dissipate quickly in the open air.

A vehicle-borne device is limited in size only by the vehicle, and may be designed to attack a structure. In order to achieve the best possible effect, the terrorist will want to get the vehicle as

PREVENT

close as possible to the structure. Because of the size of the blast caused by a vehicle-borne device, the greatest risk in built-up areas is from secondary fragmentation – things like flying glass. To protect ourselves from a large device we need not only to move away from the immediate vicinity, but also to stay away as much as possible from glazed areas.

A vehicle device can be massive and its effects can be devastating.

Biological or chemical attack

While it may be the subject of many books and films, an effective biological or chemical attack is actually tremendously difficult to achieve. It is much easier to kill or injure using explosives or arson. However, in order to explain the possibilities we will cover the basics of chemical and biological weapons.

The biggest effect of a biological or chemical attack is likely to be psychological. People have a fear of these weapons far in excess of their effect. Consider the two contemporary examples: the 1995 Sarin (nerve gas) attack on the Tokyo underground and the anthrax attack on the US postal system. In Tokyo 5,000 people were hospitalised, many as a precautionary measure, but only 11 died. In October 2001, 3 anthrax letters were circulated around the US postal system. They were handled by dozens of people and potentially exposed to hundreds, but only 2 people died. In contrast to the spread of the biological agent, fear in the USA spread like wildfire, and the response, it could be said, was entirely disproportionate to the threat. The fear created was certainly far in excess of the danger. Many of the effects of biological or chemical weapons can be treated to varying degrees, and huge sums are spent by governments on ensuring that the resources needed to respond to and clean-up after such an attack are permanently vigilant.

Chemical weapons

Chemical agents are poisons designed to work by contact, ingestion or inhalation. They are not diseases and do not make you infectious. They come in four main groups:

- *Nerve agents. These work by disrupting the central nervous system. Sarin is a nerve gas. They can be gaseous and 'non-persistent', which means that they act quickly and then dissipate; alternatively, they can be persistent, so more like a gloopy liquid that hangs around letting off a low level of gas.*

- *Blood agents. These work by assaulting the cellular structure and specifically by attacking blood cells and preventing them from carrying oxygen. Hydrogen cyanide is a blood agent.*

- **Choking agents.** These work by irritating soft membranes such as eyes and lungs. They are relatively easy to source and include chemicals like chlorine and phosgene.

- **Blister agents.** These agents attack the membranes of the nose, throat and mouth. They also leave painful blisters on the skin. They can cause large numbers of casualties, but tend not to have a high mortality rate. Examples are lewisite and mustard gas.

All these chemicals are difficult to disperse effectively. It is generally easier to create mass casualties with an explosive attack or arson.

Nuclear or radiological attack

A nuclear bomb is one where the device has a 'high yield'. Put more simply, this means the energy released is out of proportion to its size, causing astounding levels of destruction. It requires state-sponsored investment to create even simple nuclear devices.

The materials, technology and know-how needed to manufacture these devices are all controlled internationally by the nuclear non-proliferation treaty, and globally significant assets are allocated to monitoring materials and suitably qualified individuals. With the amount of effort and expense assigned to ensuring this kind of attack does not happen, the possibility that a terrorist could bring together the relevant items and know-how, import them into the country, assemble them without detection and set off the device is pretty much in the realms of fiction.

It takes state levels of funding to achieve a high-yield device.

A radiological attack or 'dirty bomb' is one where a normal explosive device is surrounded by matter that is contaminated with radiation. As with chemical and biological devices, the key aim may be to create fear. For those who are not directly injured by the explosion, the primary effect of such a device is to deny access to a particular area until the clean-up is completed. Because of the nature of radiation, this can be a long time. Remember that the actual levels of radiation involved may be very low, but if the device qualifies for the tag 'radiological', the media response will certainly create fear.

After any biological, chemical or radiological attack, the authorities will be concerned about the spread of contamination. If you have been involved in any way, they may ask you not to go home until you have been decontaminated. Special teams exist that can decontaminate large numbers of the general public. They will clean people and provide alternative clothing.

POSSIBLE TARGETS

While an attack can occur almost anywhere, it is possible to make an assessment of where the risks might be higher or lower. It is worth considering some of the locations we use or visit regularly.

Public transport including air travel

Public transport systems have always been a favoured target. They provide a high-density target for the terrorist (many people in one place), and any attack paralyses a city by discouraging workers from using the system after the event. Consider the effect of high-profile movie stars refusing to use international air travel after 9/11. Attacks in Madrid and London also show how effective this type of attack can be.

PREVENT

In terms of explosive device, public transport can really only be attacked with a carried device, which limits its size and in turn the number of casualties. While any attack is shocking and any loss of life is tragic, it is worth reflecting on the statistics – this may seem cold, but if lessons can be learned they should be. Four devices in London killed 52 people, and the thirteen devices in Madrid killed 192 people. The lesson from such grisly figures is that a single carried device, even in a confined environment, is capable of killing and seriously injuring only those in the immediate vicinity. You can greatly reduce the risks you are exposed to by creating distance or, better still, putting some form of physical barrier between you and anything you are suspicious of. For trains and buses, the terrorist will need to carry either a large explosive belt concealed by a bulky jacket or a bag containing the device.

Public transport will remain a target for terrorist organisations.

In terms of the after effect, anyone riding the relatively empty Tube trains in London through the rest of July 2005 will agree that there must have been some overall impact on the UK economy.

Despite the threat, public transport remains a safe and effective means of transport.

Because the coverage in the media has been so high profile, it is worth considering the relative risk you are exposed to on public transport; and the London Underground is a useful example. An average of 2.7 million passenger journeys are made every day on the Tube. So, even with the worst attack in its history, in 2005 the chances of being killed by a terrorist attack on the underground network were around 1 in 19 million. It is commonly accepted that the odds of winning the National Lottery are around 1 in 14 million. Compare this with the chances of being the victim of one of the 150 or so muggings every day in London or the 9 fatal car accidents in the UK and hopefully you are able to make an informed decision about whether or not you feel safe using public transport.

Air travel holds a specific attraction for the terrorist for two reasons. First, it requires a relatively small device to achieve the failure of an aircraft, killing everyone on board: on 21 December 1988 an estimated 340–450 grams of explosive caused the loss of Pan Am flight 103 over Lockerbie, resulting in 270 deaths. Secondly, if the aircraft is hijacked, it becomes a very large vehicle device capable of causing enormous destruction, as the attacks on the World Trade Center showed. Actually getting a device onto an aircraft is very difficult, and since 9/11 few passengers will have failed to notice the increased security at all airports and inside aircraft to prevent an attack.

PREVENT

Public gatherings and high-profile targets

Any event that attracts a large group of people, particularly with media coverage, is open to being targeted, so public gatherings will always be vulnerable. Attacking a high-profile target is likely to demand additional time and effort, and will pose a high risk of failure for the terrorist. Therefore, locations of political significance are less likely to be attacked as long as a wide and varied choice of easy targets, such as trains, is available. The benefits really must outweigh the potential dangers for a terrorist.

Public gatherings

The Bali bombing on 12 October 2002 killed 202 people. The attack was specifically aimed at the large number of people, known to be Westerners, in the Sari Nightclub. This venue understandably had little in the way of security against such an attack. As yet there have been no high-profile attacks in the UK or other

While they present an attractive target for the terrorist, most large public gatherings also have increased security measures.

Western countries at large public gatherings like football matches. Security at such events is particularly high and will normally include the venue being searched before the arrival of the general public and searches of everyone entering the building.

High-profile targets

Buildings or locations of political significance are always under surveillance by terrorist organisations because they offer a high prize. The attack on the Pentagon on 9/11 was never going to achieve the kind of destruction achieved in New York city centre; however, the message delivered by directly attacking the US military HQ was lost on few. We will discuss places to avoid while overseas in Chapter 7. In the UK, unless you are warned otherwise, it is pretty safe to assume that when visiting sites like the Houses of Parliament you are in a location that has been made particularly difficult to attack and is therefore inherently safe.

Infrastructure

All terrorists would like to attack the national infrastructure. This could include the oil and gas industry, the National Grid, the roads network or major air and sea ports. In the UK we have a history of protecting our infrastructure – from huge efforts to build in spare capacity during the Second World War, into the hard protection and contingency planning during the Cold War, and then our long struggle against Irish terrorism. Despite all this planning and protection, it is worth remembering that the IRA devised and was only just stopped from conducting an attack on electricity substations around London that would have had catastrophic effects on the capital's power supply. There are elements of our infrastructure that are quite finely balanced and this becomes all too apparent during periods of natural pressure. Most of our fuel

PREVENT

and food supplies operate on a 'just enough just in time' logistics system, which means that, whenever there is a threat of a flu pandemic or bad weather, people panic buy, knowing that the supply system can be relatively easily affected.

Intimidation and threats

Long-term intimidation can be a terrifying experience for the victim, and there is no doubt that the activities of some animal rights' groups fall squarely into the category of terrorism. The threat of action can also be highly effective. The 1997 Grand National was disrupted, with a cost to the economy measured in millions; the cost of the IRA operation? – 10p for the phone call. Threatening to conduct an attack can influence public behaviour, and, if the terrorist can create fear without actually having to take action, he will.

Despite our history, much of our national infrastructure operates on a fine balance and as such will remain a key target for terrorists.

The UK Government has provided high-profile advice to every home in the UK in the form of the 'Preparing for Emergencies: What You Need to Know' booklet. There are a number of websites that also offer advice, and you will find their details in the list of Websites and Sources of Further Information. In general terms, the booklet encourages you to think about what you might do in an emergency and to make some simple preparations, and it gives advice that holds good for almost any unforeseen situation: **Go in, Stay in, Tune in.**

HM Government

PREPARING FOR EMERGENCIES
WHAT YOU NEED TO KNOW

The Government wouldn't have spent the money on issuing every home and business with a 'Preparing for Emergencies' booklet unless the threat was real. Have a plan to deal with emergencies.

Contacting friends and family

Anyone who had a relative or friend in London on 7 July 2005 will know that, during times of increased use, the mobile phone network tends to crash. If you have ever tried to call someone on a mobile on New Year's Eve, you will have experienced the frustration. For many people the stress of not knowing the fate of a friend or loved one can be significant. Even if your loved ones are nowhere near an incident, you still want to confirm their safety. So, as most people will reach for a mobile, the best course of action is actually to use a landline or email. Wherever you work, discuss how you will contact your partner or family in the event of an incident. If you both work in offices that are likely to be evacuated, perhaps you could agree that you will both call a relative who is always at home. Whatever you decide, make a plan today for how you will contact your loved ones in the event of an incident and stick to it.

PREVENT

Useful things to know at work or at home

Make sure you know the following:

- **Where and how to turn off the water, gas and electricity in your home.** *Do not rely on one person to know how to do this. If someone is trusted to be at home alone (for example, a teenager), he or she should be told how to switch things off in an emergency.*

 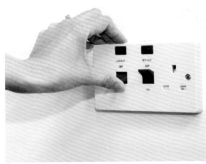

Ensure everyone in your home knows how to turn off the water, gas and electricity.

- **The emergency procedures for your children at school.** *Discuss this with your partner. If you are both at work and cannot contact each other or the school, what is your 'default' agreement? Your school will look after your children until you arrive, so perhaps the best solution might be to wait until traffic has reduced and then collect them.*

- **The emergency procedures in your workplace.** *What is the fire evacuation plan and is there a different plan for a terrorist attack? Is there an alternative evacuation route or a safe location within your building?*

● **If any elderly or vulnerable neighbours might need your help.** They may be particularly stressed and need reassurance.

● **How to tune into your local radio station.** National stations will give you general advice, but local stations will give information on specific details in your area. More importantly, do you have a radio that will work on batteries? And the batteries?

Useful things to have at work or at home

Things to have during an emergency fall into three categories: those you will need to gather at the time and that you probably use in daily life; those you can keep in an emergencies cupboard; and finally a supply of food and water.

Items to gather at the time

○ house and car keys

○ mobile phone and charger

○ all cash and credit cards

○ some extra clothes

As an emergency starts to unfold, gather together your day kit and items that you can carry in your pockets.

PREVENT

Items in your emergency box or cupboard

- a list of key phone numbers
  - local police station
  - doctor
  - work
  - school
  - friends and family

- toiletries, sanitary supplies and spare regular medication

- battery-operated radio and spare batteries

- battery-operated torch and spare batteries

- candles and lighter or matches

- home first-aid kit and blankets

Having an emergency box is sensible for a number of reasons and you will find it useful on a surprisingly regular basis.

Items in your food cupboard

- tinned foods and a tin opener

- bottled water, at least 2 litres per person per day, so as much as you can store

- long-life or powdered milk for making tea

- if you are happy to use it, a camping stove for heating food or water

Keeping a food box can also help in rotating your long-storage supplies.

Gathering all this equipment could seem a bit over the top and perhaps paranoid; however, it is always worth having. Power cuts and everyday bumps and scrapes mean that torches, candles and first-aid kits are a must for every home. Keeping tinned food can seem pointless, but it serves more than one purpose. During the winter, the supply of food to supermarkets can be affected for short periods by bad weather or illness. The government accepts that in such a situation no one would go hungry but there would be panic buying. So you can either resign yourself to doing battle with the panic-buying masses in the aisles of your local superstore, or ride out the storm for a few days by eating your supply of long-life foods. The choice is yours.

Useful things to have on your person

Chapter 1 covered what to carry in your everyday kit and established that it is always sensible to have your mobile phone with you. Another very useful item is a credit-card-sized crib sheet containing important numbers and your family's plan in case something goes wrong – that is, arrangements for getting in touch. These are easily made by laminating a small piece of paper.

A simple family contact card prevents confusion when there is an emergency.

PREVENT

If asked to leave your home

In the worst case, during an emergency you may be asked to leave your home. If you are given plenty of warning, then you can take time to consider what you will load into your car. If, however, you are asked to leave quickly, consider the following:

- *Turn off all gas, electricity and water, and unplug your appliances.*

- *Ensure your home is left secure – i.e. doors and windows locked.*

- *If you are able to take your car, take water and blankets and tune into your local radio station. (Of course, if you equip your car as we discussed in Chapter 2, it will already be stocked with water and blankets.)*

WHAT WILL THE AUTHORITIES BE DOING?

Understanding what in general terms the authorities are likely to be doing during an incident will reduce the uncertainty that is the main fuel for fear. Some in British politics have criticised, perhaps unfairly, the UK's response to emergencies. In fact, it is a widely held opinion internationally that the UK has put in place some of the best plans in the world for responding to terrorist incidents. So don't believe everything you read in the papers. In addition to the blue flashing lights you see on the streets, a huge organisation exists in the UK to deal with emergencies and emergency planning. The UK also has some of the best low-profile counter-terrorist assets in the world, whose very *raison d'être* is to deal with the terrorist threat to the UK.

The Civil Contingencies Act 2004 established a consistent level of civil protection activity across the UK. You can read a copy and

SILVER

OUTER

INNER CO

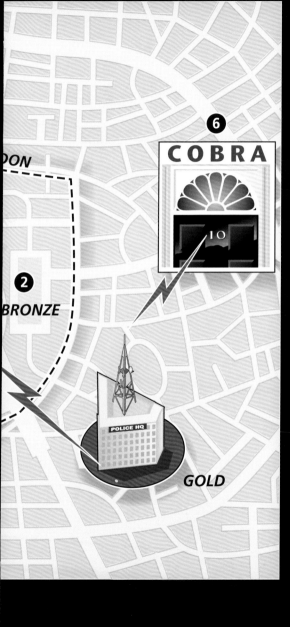

1. At the scene, the emergency services will deal with the immediate casualties, clean up and start gathering evidence

2. The Bronze level of command controls the task site and runs the inner cordon

3. The emergency services may set up a casualty handling area inside the outer cordon to prioritise who goes to hospital first

4. If there is a fear of contamination, you may be asked to remain in the outer cordon until you have been decontaminated

5. Silver Command controls entrance into the outer cordon and will ensure the team running Bronze has everything it needs

6. Gold Command will be set up somewhere like a police HQ, and in some cases will report direct to the Cabinet Office Briefing Room (COBRA)

other information relating to civil defence on the government's 'UK resilience' website, the details of which are in the list of Websites and Sources of Further Information.

In outline, the Act defines that there are six activities that should be conducted to ensure an integrated approach to emergency planning. They are:

1. anticipation
2. assessment
3. prevention
4. preparation
5. response
6. recovery management

There are also duties specifically assigned to the authorities, including:

- risk assessment

- business continuity management (BCM)

- emergency planning

- maintaining public awareness

While programmes like Spooks are not exactly factual, it is worth remembering that there are a large number of people who are highly trained and paid specifically to keep you safe.

In addition, your local authority is specifically required to cooperate and share information.

All of this is, I'm afraid, rather dry, but the lesson to take away is that there is a large chunk of legislation and significant planning activity involved in preparing for an emergency. We will focus now on the emergency response.

PREVENT

Who will be helping?

The authorities will become aware of most incidents through an initial 999 call, and from this they are able immediately to task the Police, Fire Brigade, Ambulance, Coastguard, Mountain Rescue or Army Bomb Disposal Teams as appropriate. As soon as it becomes apparent that an emergency is unfolding, a well-oiled and exercised system is put into play. The actions required during a major incident are designed to be similar to those that emergency services use for smaller incidents, thus ensuring that everyone is familiar with what they are supposed to be doing.

In terms of who will be assisting, there are those who are referred to as Level 1 responders – those who would normally be involved in an emergency, such as the emergency services; and others referred to as Level 2 responders – those who may be required for a specific emergency, for example, utilities providers. Level 2 responders also include a number of volunteer organisations that are permanently ready to assist – people like the St John Ambulance, who are called upon to prepare mass casualty-handling locations in major incidents. The emergency services can call on just about any individual or agency to assist them during a terrorist incident and have powers to encourage people to play their part.

The actions in the immediate aftermath of a major incident are well practised. The UK has some of the best emergency services in the world.

How will the response be controlled?

During any incident the authorities will establish a tier of multi-agency emergency management:

- Bronze Command – Operational Level

- Silver Command – Tactical Level

- Gold Command – Strategic Level

The Bronze level of command will be set up at the scene, and its job is to get on with the business of saving lives and dealing with the intimate details of the incident. In the UK, the system is organised according to a 'bottom-up' approach. This means that the front-line workers identify problems, report the situation up the chain of command and request additional assistance. Bronze will normally also establish what may be referred to as a Forward Control Point. This will control access into an inner cordon.

The Silver level of command exists to ensure that Bronze is acting in an efficient and effective manner. In a large incident it will be established either near or adjacent to the incident scene and will probably control access into the outer cordon. Silver is able to coordinate bringing assets to and from the area of the incident and look at the wider implications of the emergency.

If there is a requirement for a higher level of decision making and coordination, the Gold level of command may be established. This is based around what is referred to as the Strategic Coordinating Group. Basically it comprises the bosses of all the emergency services and other relevant management, who come together to provide strategic direction and decision making. Gold Command will be set up in somewhere like a Police Force HQ building.

COBRA

Should the incident be of national importance, it is the Gold level of command that will report to the Cabinet Office Briefing Room, also known as COBRA.

PREVENT

During a major incident, the highest political levels will be informed of what is happening and involved in deciding what level of response is required.

So, because a framework of decision making is used that is generic to all areas of the UK, every part responds in a similar way and is also able to request assistance from regional or national resources. There are regular exercises, particularly in London, to practise not only the command and control of the response but also more specialist skills – for example, decontamination after a chemical incident.

REDUCING RISK: IF YOU ARE INVOLVED

The chances of being involved in a terrorist incident are tiny. Therefore, you shouldn't have to change your lifestyle significantly to stay safe. Any advice that asks you to do something that does not feel natural to you will fail; you should develop safe habits and keep to them. Most of what you will find in the rest of this chapter is common-sense advice that you should employ every day.

If you are involved in a terrorist or major incident, the chances are that your instincts will take over. There is a weight of evidence that people who are trained to deal with high-stress situations, such as soldiers and members of the emergency services, have a higher survival rate in such instances. By considering the actions you might take before such an incident

Soldiers and members of the emergency services tend to react better in crisis situations. By developing your understanding and being aware of your surroundings, you too can increase your own safety.

occurs, you can hopefully influence your instinctive reaction and reduce the risk you expose yourself to.

If you are involved, then you can expect the emergency services to be on hand rapidly. They will want you to evacuate the immediate area, but may ask you to stay within an outer cordon. If you have been contaminated, or perhaps can give evidence after witnessing something, then you may be required to stay in the area for some time. If no one is available to offer you advice, then move away quickly from where you think the greatest danger is to a place you feel safe. Do not leave the general area until you are sure it is sensible for you to do so.

At work

Wherever you work, ensure that you know the evacuation procedures and contingency plans for emergencies. In addition to this, make sure you are familiar with the contents of your work space. This means that, if you are asked to search your building, you will be able to tell quickly whether something is out of place. Pay attention to people moving through your workplace. If they are delivering something, has it been signed for and accepted? If it is possible to walk into your office without going through a security check, are they actually looking for unattended belongings? Remember that your company may be at risk from threats other than terrorism; you would be surprised at the size of the industry that discovers the activities of people's competitors.

If you are the boss of a company, or have responsibilities for the security of your business and employees, the government provides lots of advice and assistance if you look for it. The Security Service (MI5) gives general advice to businesses, and if you use an IT system or network, then the National Infrastructure Coordination Centre (NICSS) may be able to offer you some assistance as well. Details of both are in the list of Websites and Sources of Further Information.

Modern office block construction

If you work in an office block that has been built since the mid-1960s, it is likely that the construction has a number of common design factors. The strength of the building will be derived from a steel frame, but there will also be a significant amount of reinforced concrete running through the centre of the structure and immediately adjacent to the lifts and stairwells. The exterior skin of the building will include large amounts of glass, and there will probably be either an underground car park or service areas below ground level.

The two primary features to be aware of in most modern office blocks are a central concrete core and an abundance of glass.

Whatever type of building you work in and particularly if it has significant quantities of internal glazing, it is worth being familiar with the evacuation plan and the protocols for what happens in the event of an emergency. You will normally find these at the reception or security desk. In many buildings there is a single evacuation plan for all eventualities. Evacuating to the

out if your office windows are fitted with anti-shatter
or blast net curtains; 90 per cent of casualties caused by
bombs are victims of flying glass

desk by the window is not the best place to watch an
lding drama in the city; get away from the windows and
isk of flying glass

and practise getting all your colleagues safely out of the
ling in an emergency

(4) *You should be familiar with the building fire and security plans*

(5) *Make your building security staff aware of any suspicious vehicles*

(6) *Know where all your fire exits are, not just the nearest exit*

(7) *Know where your nearest safe haven is; this is normally a stairwell or similar, with no windows*

outside fire assembly point when there is about to be a large explosion might not be the best course of action, so don't be afraid to ask questions now about emergency plans. In many situations there are few places safer than the underground car park of a large office block, so you should feel confident about the building's emergency protocols before you leave that place of relative safety.

It is sensible to consider the risks that you, specifically, are exposed to. During bomb attacks in built-up areas, most injuries are caused by flying glass. Unless you work in a building where your employers have fitted bomb film, flying glass should be your primary concern. You can tell if bomb film is fitted either by asking your building facilities team or by looking at the corner of a window pane for the edges of the film sheet; it looks a bit like a big sheet of sticky tape. Some modern triple-glazed panes are also designed to withstand blast without film. Even if you do have protected glazing, be aware that, under extreme conditions, bomb

Stairwells tend to be the most structurally sound areas in a modern office block.

film simply converts small shards of flying glass into large sheets of flying glass, so protecting yourself from glazing should still be a priority.

Decide what actions you will take if you become aware of an incident developing. Your first action should be to move to a place of intermediate safety. This will be the nearest place that offers protection from flying glass. It should also be away from exterior doors. This location should have at least one solid wall separating you from the exterior skin of the building. Stairwells are normally a good choice, as they routinely take you directly to the basement and are sound parts of any modern structure. Once in your relative place of safety, you can decide what to do next.

PREVENT

In some modern complexes, leaving your floor might involve entering a central glazed atrium. In this instance you may decide to stay where you are until you know that it is safe to evacuate. Once at floor or basement level, you should decide whether to evacuate the building or to remain where you are. Your building supervisor will no doubt offer advice, but remember, if an incident is developing in nearby streets, you may be safer in the basement car park than you are outside. Once again, familiarity with, and confidence in, the building emergency plans will help you make sound decisions.

In any type of incident, be it fire or security alert, do not use the lifts. If you find using stairs difficult or impossible, identify someone in your workplace who is willing to assist you and spend some time together practising using the stairs.

Public transport

Situational awareness was discussed in Chapter 1. When using public transport, you should be particularly aware of the environment around you. Certainly being alert will enable you to reduce the risk you are exposed to from threats like petty thieves and groups of drunken youths. Unfortunately, there is no generic

While statistically speaking it is safe to use public transport, you should remain aware of the environment around you.

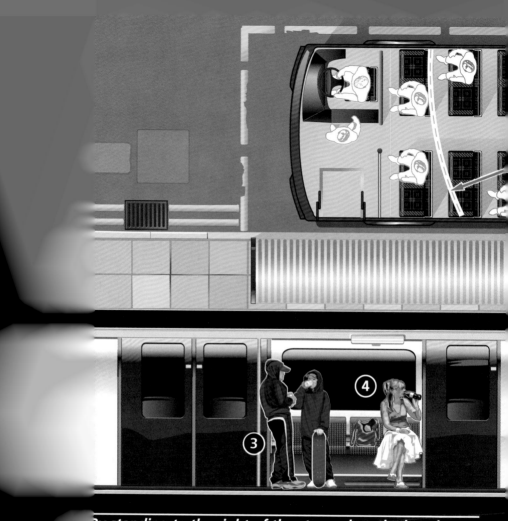

By standing to the right of the stop, when the bus draws up you can observe the passengers before entering

Do your '5 and 20s': once you are sitting down, establish what is in the immediate area around you out to 5 feet, and then in less detail who and what is within 20 feet

Keep an eye out for pickpockets, who may be operating in pairs or groups

Keep your bags closed and secured and if possible within

(5) Most mobile phone theft and other street crime i...
on youth; it is sensible to keep an eye on these g...

(6) There are many reasons someone might be nervo...
you're really uncomfortable, then have the confid...
move seats or carriage

(7) Do not be driven by racial stereotypes; there is n...
standard profile for a terrorist

(8) If you wouldn't feel comfortable with a £100 note...
your hand, don't hold a phone; wait to make you...

Do not allow yourself to be drawn to media-fuelled stereotypes about suicide bombers. Look for nervous or unusual behaviour and unusually bulky clothing during hot weather.

profile that applies to the terrorist, so do not be tempted to focus your attention on any particular ethnic or religious group. Al Qaeda has deliberately used operators who live a fully Western lifestyle so they cannot easily be identified as extremists. About the only common factor in terrorist attacks in the UK is that most of them have been committed by relatively young men.

Boarding public transport

When buses arrive at a bus stop, it is possible to view the passengers before you get in, so take the opportunity to do so. If a bus turns up full of rowdy football supporters, you might decide to wait and take the next one. If one turns up and for whatever reason you feel uncomfortable about someone or something on board, then surely it is sensible to wait for the next bus. If you do spot something, but decide to board anyway, sitting nearest the driver is normally the safest option, as you can tell him if something really concerns you.

When boarding a train, always try to board a carriage that you have looked at first. This is easily achieved by allowing the carriage to pass you and then entering at the rear. With a stationary train, walk past the carriage you want to enter and then walk back through it to find a seat. You should always keep your belongings with you if possible. If you have a large bag and have to leave it in the baggage space at the carriage entrance, try to sit as close to it as you can. Wherever you are, ensure you are facing your bags.

Doing a '5 and 20'

Once you have found your seat, conduct a quick visual check of the area around you. You probably do this subconsciously anyway, but we will call it a '5 and 20'. This means that you look first in the immediate 5 feet of where you are sitting: under the seat, who is sitting next to you and immediately in front and behind you. Then settle into your chair. Once you are comfortable, you can then conduct a slower visual check of the 20 feet around you. Are there any unattended bags? Is there something out of place, like a panel of the carriage that has been forced open? Does anyone look particularly stressed?

There are many reasons why someone could be agitated or stressed, and it would be senseless to panic every time you saw someone sweating and looking nervous. Once something attracts your eye, try to look for other linking factors that may then lead you to take action. Your action might simply be to move seat, or to make someone aware of your concerns.

Once you have conducted your '5 and 20' check, you can then identify all the emergency exits in your area and ensure you know the location of things like the hammers for getting through the windows in an emergency. All trains now have safety information cards on them; take a moment to see what advice they give. Many trains are fitted with complex safety systems, and reading the card will provide you with information that your instincts will act upon should there be an incident.

Incidents on public transport

If you do find yourself on public transport during a major incident or terrorist attack, then try to do the following:

- *While the incident is in progress, try to hold on to something and get yourself in a low-down and braced position. Do not let go or allow yourself to come out of the brace until absolutely everything has stopped moving.*

- *Once things have stopped moving, orient yourself. Ensure you have properly identified the quickest route out before you head off. Evidence shows that, in a significant proportion of such incidents, people spend long periods of time lost in wreckage because they did not orient themselves to their environment. An upside-down railway carriage looks very different from one the right way up, so take your time to get this right.*

- *Escape by the quickest route and move away from the immediate area. Do not leave the general area until told to do so by the emergency services.*

If you are injured, you need to make a decision about whether to stay where you are and await rescue or try to escape, understanding that you may cause yourself more harm. This will normally be a relatively simple decision; if you are able to escape with an injury, do so.

PREVENT

Large gatherings

Events such as football matches and concerts are very difficult for a terrorist to target, but should you be involved in an incident, then following some simple advice can make a huge amount of difference. There is little you can do about reducing the risk of an event being targeted or about your location within a venue, so most of the advice is related to how to move in a crowd and how to escape safely.

Modern venues are constructed using complex crowd dynamics programmes that ensure evacuation can be quick and efficient. Unfortunately, the best planning in the world cannot account for the self-serving actions of a fear-filled crowd. Once again, situational awareness is key. Know where the nearest fire exits are when you are in a venue. Sometimes these are not the way you came in – for example, at all football stadiums in the UK it is always possible to evacuate onto the pitch and then out of the

If you are going to a large sporting event or gathering with friends or family, agree a meeting point should you get separated.

stadium using wider, vehicle access routes. If you are with a group, particularly if you are with children, try to stay together. Agree immediately on a meeting point outside the venue, so that, if you do get separated, you can find each other quickly. This should not be in the immediate vicinity of the exits.

Rather than heading directly for the exits, you may be better to aim for a wall or barrier. By doing this you can maintain an immovable object on one side of you that you can use as protection. You also avoid the 'rush and crush' that can be experienced in the funnel immediately around an exit, and come at an exit from an angle. If you feel the immediate threat has already passed, you may decide that becoming involved in the crush serves no purpose and that you are safer to wait until the crush has passed. If you do find yourself in the middle of a crowd, stay on your feet and try to create a space for yourself. Most importantly, protect the area around your chest so that you can breathe. This can be achieved easily by folding your arms in front of your chest and bracing them.

Places of safety

Once you have moved away from the immediate area of any major incident or terrorist attack, make for a place of safety. Obviously your initial instinct will probably be to go home, but it may not be the simplest or safest option. If you walk or cycle, then you may find it relatively easy to get home. However, if you use a car or public transport, the chances are that the system will be under significant pressure. You have two options: join the crowded buses and roads, or find a place of safety and wait out the rush.

'Hard' places of safety are those that you might go to during an attack; these include any area with limited glazing and no thin wall to the outside world – for example, underground car parks, the central reinforced concrete stairwells of many office blocks and locations like cinema theatres.

PREVENT

A hotel lobby is a 'soft' place of safety off the street.

A 'soft' place of safety is somewhere you might go to wait for the end of the rush of everyone trying to get home. Basically, you need somewhere comfortable to get off the streets and wait for the situation to pass. This might include a friend's home, or in a big city is more likely to be a bar, café or hotel lobby. Wherever you go, consider calmly whether there is likely to be any further threat and, if so, whether you are likely to be in the area concerned.

How to get information

During any major incident it always takes a while to form a picture of what has actually happened. Comparing initial press releases with the final report on an incident is always interesting, as they are routinely wildly different. The lesson is to concentrate on the implications of an incident rather than the actual incident itself. For example, whether there was a bomb or a gas leak is not relevant to you; whether the railway line you use to get home is working or not is very relevant.

The best source of information is local radio. National news and radio reports will tend to focus on the incident and what is being done at the site itself. Local radio will obviously cover this, but has an obligation to inform listeners about things such as public-

The police have a lot to do in the aftermath of an incident. Try not to expect too much if you are not involved.

transport changes and school-collection plans. Make sure you know the frequency of your local radio station where you work and at home and record it on your crib sheet.

Please also spare a thought for the PC tasked to provide a high-profile presence at your Tube station. While the police and emergency services will have the best overall understanding of what is going on, that does not mean the PC on the streets has been told any more than the media.

If there are significant casualties, the police will very quickly establish a casualty hotline. Please call this only once you are sure that your loved ones are missing or if you know they will have been in the immediate area of the incident.

Information on how to find your local radio station and information about public transport can be found in the list of Websites and Sources of Further Information.

Post-incident debriefing

If you are unlucky enough to have been involved in a major incident or have witnessed horrific injuries, then you should seek advice about post-incident counselling. A long time ago this activity used to carry a stigma in the emergency services and military, and many people felt that if you needed to talk about something after it happened you were 'soft'. Thankfully a more sensible attitude now prevails. Having been through the process myself, I found it entirely enjoyable – far less like seeing a 'trick cyclist' and more like having a chat over some free tea and biscuits! If, for whatever reason, you decide not to approach someone after being involved in a traumatic incident, then the following may be of use:

PREVENT

- *Try to get together with someone who was involved in the same or a similar experience to you. This could be a friend who you know has been in a nasty car crash. Find somewhere you can have a chat without being interrupted. This might be at home with a cup of tea or over a drink in a quiet pub.*

- *With that person talk through the detailed events of the day. Ensure you start by talking about your day before the incident and what you were thinking about.*

- *Discuss what you saw in detail and how it made you feel.*

- *Discuss what happened after the incident and whether you have any regrets or wishes about what you did or how the event unfolded.*

- *Accept that it is quite normal to find that, in the days following an incident, your sleep may be interrupted and you may find yourself dwelling on the incident during the day. Problems arise when people ignore these symptoms. Such thoughts are entirely normal and subside quite quickly.*

Talking things through normally helps in the long run.

- *The key thing to remember is that any symptoms are easily dealt with if you resolve them quickly. The longer you leave it, the harder it is to deal with trauma.*

There are many support groups that deal with people who might be suffering from post-traumatic stress disorder; you will find details in the list of Websites and Sources of Further Information.

How to get information

If you are not directly involved in a terrorist attack or major incident, it is probable that your attention will turn immediately to the safety of your close family, then to your close friends and then to acquaintances who may be directly involved. This desire first to confirm the safety of your close circle and then to find some link to the incident in your wider network is a natural reaction.

Making contact with your immediate family should be easy, as you will by now have an established protocol for the family to get in touch with one another.

While you are confirming that everyone is OK, it is sensible to follow the government advice: **Go in, Stay in, Tune in.** Tune your radio to the local station and listen for details of school closures or public-transport arrangements. By doing this you will also be able to tell if your loved ones are going to be home late and therefore not worry when they don't appear at the normal time.

If you want the bigger picture, then national TV stations are the obvious choice. Remember that you should always keep an ear to the local radio, as it will be used by the authorities to inform you of specific details for your area.

If you have confirmed that all your loved ones are well and are established in your home with the radio tuned in, perhaps now is the time to show a little community spirit. There may be people living near you who will not be aware of the situation or who might be worrying about loved ones. Perhaps you could help. Consider visiting elderly neighbours to see if they need any help. During the immediate aftermath of a terrorist or major incident, it is important to establish a link with your neighbours. They can be a useful source of information.

PREVENT

Places of safety

If you are not directly involved, your primary place of safety will be your home. Wherever you are, once again the clear advice is: **Go in, Stay in, Tune in.** If it becomes apparent that you may suffer loss of services to your home, then early action could make things easier. Below you will find some general advice on what to do if your home is affected by an incident.

Water

Try to fill your bath with cold water. This will ensure you have drinking water if your supply is cut off. If the water is already cut off, you may be able to drain your hot water tank (if you have one) into the bath. This water should really be boiled before drinking. In either case, having a bath full of water serves a number of purposes. During an electricity cut you may use candles or perhaps a camping stove for the first time. A towel quickly soaked in the bath acts as an excellent fire blanket and can quickly stop a minor candle problem developing into a major house fire.

Filling your bath might save you from a number of trips to a stand pipe.

Electrical appliances

If the power has been turned off, unplug all your electrical appliances and disconnect any aerials. You will need to think about what to do with the contents of your fridge and freezer. Avoid opening them unless you absolutely have to. During a typical British winter, it is possible on most days to find a spot outside and in the shade that is a similar temperature to your refrigerator. Your freezer is a well-insulated box and, unless there are freezing conditions outside, the best course of action is to leave your freezer to defrost slowly, but to use the food in it as soon as possible. During the summer months the contents of your refrigerator will quickly become warm, and you should strongly consider whether it is really worth increasing the load on the medical system by trying that 'only slightly off' milk.

Try not to open your fridge or freezer during a power cut.

Please don't . . .

During the immediate aftermath of a terrorist incident, the police will be putting significant resources into trying to prevent any further attack. It is likely that, while the emergency services are dealing with the immediate scene, others may be conducting raids or providing a high-profile presence at other potential targets. During this initial period you can help the police by helping yourself. There are a few things that certainly add to the stress of police work, so please consider the following:

- *Dialling 999 is for emergencies when an immediate response is required. Please **don't** call 999 to report that you are unable to get in contact with a loved one or to find out what is going on. This sounds sensible, but consider that, of the 2.5 million 999 calls received by*

PREVENT

the Met in 2005, only 20 per cent related to emergencies needing an immediate response. **Do** dial 999 if you see something suspicious or believe you have information that is of immediate relevance to any follow-up action.

- The police presence at your railway station or airport is there to deter a further attack and to maintain vigilance. Try to resist your desire to engage them in conversation and ask if they know what is going on at the incident site. They probably know less than you.

- Speculating about what may or may not have happened is counterproductive and can cause distress to people who may have relatives involved in an incident. Please try not to gossip about casualties or the areas concerned. In conversation, be meticulous about what you say and explain the source of your information. This sounds overly cautious, but experience in these incidents shows that some of the worst distress can be caused by simple misinformation and misunderstanding. Consider the following: a hypothetical blast near an office block in central London injures between twenty and thirty people, but no one is killed. The radio reports that hundreds **could** have been killed. Someone relating the story says: 'There's been a bomb in central London and hundreds might have been killed.' Anyone with a friend or relative in central London is now needlessly very concerned. At the extreme end of emotional response, people may even fall into shock. I have seen this kind of unintentional misinformation at first hand. It is entirely avoidable if people think before they speak.

CHAPTER SIX

Global Crime

If you're travelling off the beaten track, you need to be prepared to see things you might not agree with.

In general terms, the best way to avoid becoming a victim of crime while overseas is to employ the patterns of behaviour we have already covered. In short, increase your situational awareness so that you can **PRE-EMPT** any trouble, **PREVENT** your involvement and if necessary **PROTECT** yourself. However, there are some specific safety issues to consider when travelling, and you will see that not everything in this chapter is crime related. Putting in place the framework of the right insurance, carrying a first-aid pack and considering where to eat and drink on holiday will ensure you are managing the risks you will meet abroad.

If you are travelling for the first time outside the normal tourist areas and the confines of the 'first world', remember that we in the UK live in a relatively crime-free society and that you may be shocked by the brutality that exists in some parts of the wider world, where crime and crime countermeasures may be very visible. For example, in many

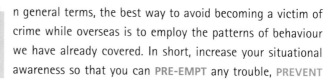

PREVENT

parts of the world it is normal for petrol stations and shops to have armed guards who will be happy to shoot first and ask questions later. Street dwellers may be treated almost as sub-human, the sex trade may be open and disturbing, and bribery may be an expected means of gaining passage. In most cases, taking the moral high ground and explaining to people that their way of life is wrong is probably not the safest course of action.

Part of travelling abroad is experiencing differing cultures and ways of life. To a certain extent, the more you are prepared to fit in, the less likely you are to become a victim.

PRE-TRAVEL ADVICE AND PLANNING

Research

No doubt you will have done some research about the place you are travelling to. If you haven't, it's always worth buying a guide-book before you leave. If nothing else, it will give you something interesting to read on the journey. More importantly, guidebooks contain advice about which areas of a city or country might not be particularly tourist friendly and will also highlight anything you ought to know about the legal system, including criminal offences that you might not be aware of. This is particularly important in relation to drug offences; in many countries the general appear-ance might be that casual drug use is acceptable, but the legal system may impose very hefty fines, prison sentences or even the death penalty.

It is also worth ensuring you are fully familiar with any religious (which may also be legal) or social taboos. If you are travelling to an Islamic state that requires women to cover their heads, ensure you are suitably prepared. These laws normally also prevent women from driving or taking part in certain other activities, such as attending sporting events or specific public

gatherings. Views on equality held in the UK are fine, but if you want to avoid becoming a criminal yourself, you should respect and conform to local laws and customs.

Before you embark upon your trip overseas, whether it is a year-long, round-the-world epic or a weekend visit to Eastern Europe, it is always worth making a quick check to ensure everything is as you expect it to be. Many countries do not have the stable political system we have here, and things can deteriorate rapidly. The Foreign & Commonwealth Office (see the details in the list of Websites and Sources of Further Information) is probably the best freely available source of information in the world. If the FCO website advises against travel, it is for a good reason,

It is always worth doing a little research before you travel. It is particularly sensible always to check the FCO website before leaving the country.

and you should be aware that most insurance companies will not cover you if you go against FCO advice. The website also includes recent reports about terrorist activity and information about local consulates.

Once you have arrived at your destination, take the time initially to gauge whether what you have read is accurate. A chat with your hotel barman or receptionist to confirm which are the less safe areas of town, how much to expect to pay for taxis and the local emergency service numbers is always time well spent.

PREVENT

Take the opportunity initially to confirm which areas are safe, which transport to use and whether there is any particular way tourists are targeted.

Packing lists and useful items

Packing routines are very personal. I like to leave it until relatively late and then lay everything out on a bed before packing. It tends to take me an hour at the most. On the other hand, I have friends who start packing for an overseas trip a month in advance and have to pack and repack at least three or four times before they feel happy. Whatever your methodology, consider the following.

Clothing

Try not to look like the ignorant tourist. The chances are you'll attract the wrong kind of attention.

If you can, try not to look like a tourist while you are on holiday. Choose clothes and items that are comfortable but not flashy, and avoid items with clearly expensive labels or English slogans. Also consider what kind of watch and jewellery to take. If it is of significant value or sentimental importance, do you really need to take it? It may be safer left at home.

PREVENT

Money

Wherever you go, it is worth considering what combination of cards, cash and travellers' cheques will best spread the risk. Credit and debit cards will work in most cashpoints around the world, but it is worth checking what bank charges you can expect before you travel. Likewise, travellers' cheques are a fantastic tool, but ensure you investigate where you can cash them in before you travel and that they have been signed by the bank. Finally, consider what cash to take. In many countries US dollars are actually more welcome than the local currency, and in areas close to the EU the euro is becoming a welcome bartering tool, particularly because the large denomination notes are sought after as an easy way to move currency.

A money belt is a sound investment if you are travelling with large amounts of cash.

Consider how you will carry your cash and what split you will make between your wallet, a concealed belt and perhaps a separate stash in a bag or hotel safe.

Your wallet needs to be cut down to the minimum before you travel: there is little point taking your Tesco Clubcard and gym membership with you if you are travelling to sub-Saharan Africa. In addition to the wallet that you will carry in a pocket or bag, consider investing in a concealed wallet or belt for your other cash, cards or travellers' cheques. There are many possibilities, but the key is to buy something that is comfortable to wear but easily concealed.

If you are travelling to a location where muggings are common, then it is worth considering carrying a dummy wallet. This should have some cash in it and perhaps a couple of your cards; not credit or payment cards but something to make it look used, like a membership card or telephone payment card. You can then try to offload this if you are mugged. It must contain enough cash to keep a mugger happy, so consider keeping a small amount of US dollars and a small amount of local currency in such a wallet. It is worth mentioning that this is obviously a potentially high-risk course of action; if it doesn't work, you may end up angering someone who probably has the upper hand. It is, though, a useful strategy in very high-risk areas.

Finally, you may want to have some kind of container put into a hotel safe. It is always useful to have some unexpected item in which cash can easily be concealed.

Documentation

You must ensure that you travel with the correct documentation and that it is available where and when you need it.

A number of documents are essential for travel. These include:

- *passport and visas and photocopies of both*

- *second means of photo ID*

- *photocopy or details of credit cards or travellers' cheques with emergency phone numbers*

- *details of any tour operator or tickets you have bought and the agent*

- *travel insurance details*

- *European Health Insurance Card (EHIC) and photocopy*

- *doctor's prescriptions for any drugs you are carrying*

PREVENT

There are a number of options for carrying all these, but the simplest is as follows.

While travelling to your destination, keep your wallet, money belt and passport together with your visa and your travel insurance original documentation on your person. This could be in a bum bag, pocket or handbag. Once you arrive at a destination, secure the original passports and insurance documents in the hotel safe and carry the copies about your person.

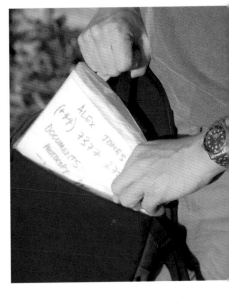

Keep the originals of the other documentation in your hand luggage or shoulder bag at all times.

Finally, before you travel, take a photocopy of all the documentation, including everything on the list, and secure it in a waterproof bag. Store this in your luggage where it will not be easily found and will not fall out – for example, within the frame space of a rucksack. That way you will always have a full copy of everything you need.

Keep a copy of all your key documentation in a waterproof bag and secure it safely in your kit.

This all sounds overly cautious, but the peace of mind of knowing you are covered should anything untoward happen is tremendously satisfying.

Medical issues

You can gain initial medical advice on travel from the NHS website (see the list of Websites and Sources of Further Information). However, as a rule you should visit your GP six weeks before travelling to ensure you receive the correct jabs and if necessary malarial treatments. If you have any prescribed medical needs, ensure you take enough for your whole trip, and, most importantly, that you have a copy of the doctor's prescription with you. To prevent any confusion, always keep any drugs you use in your hand luggage and obviously do not allow anyone else to use them.

If you are travelling in the European Union, then you need to get an EHIC card, which has replaced the E111 form. You can find advice on the NHS website.

While overseas, your body is bombarded by many different bugs and diseases. Even the most careful preparation cannot absolutely prevent a case of Delhi belly, but the best advice is to ensure your hygiene routine is good. None of this is rocket science, but not conforming to a good hygiene routine is the primary cause of most illnesses while abroad. Drink plenty of water and ensure you know it is from a good source – being fully hydrated, particularly in hotter climates, is essential if your body is to fight off the new bugs it is exposed to. Wash your hands before and after eating and after bodily functions. If you can, make a point of having a good wash every day, no matter where you are. This sounds overly simplistic, but it is worth considering that, even with draconian hygiene procedures, the most common reason for military casualties in the recent conflicts in Iraq and Afghanistan has been not

Personal hygiene is vital when travelling.

PREVENT

enemy action but dehydration, normally associated with diarrhoea and vomiting from oral ingestion of 'bugs' – so wash your hands!

If you engage in any sexual practices, it is completely unacceptable to do so without using a condom. Sexually transmitted infections are not only rife in the places you might expect like Africa. Parts of Western Europe and unsurprisingly the Balearic holiday destinations have levels of infection that are astonishing. There is no excuse for having unprotected sex.

The most common ailment for the UK tourist going overseas is still sunburn. It is incredible that, despite the years of education about skin cancer and its dangers, so many of the UK population still get burned. It is particularly worrying that people still allow their children to get sunburned. You have a responsibility to protect your children from the sun. So **don't** be a victim. Australia has the highest incidence of skin cancer in the world. Its health professionals have been giving the following simple advice for years: **slip, slop, slap, wrap!**

slip
on a shirt

slop
on sunscreen

slap
on a hat and

wrap
on sunglasses

First-aid kits

Finally, it is worth considering having your own first-aid kit, which needs to be tailored for your destination. Whoever you are and wherever you are going, you should take a basic first-aid kit.

Basic first-aid kit

- *pain relief for headaches and other low-level pain*

- *diarrhoea treatment and some electrolyte sachets*

- *selection of plasters*

- *antiseptic wipes and cream for bites or cuts*

- *insect repellent*

- *sunscreen and after-sun (make sure your sunscreen has a decent SPF level, 10 or above)*

A simple first-aid kit is essential for the traveller.

If you are going on an expedition or to a genuinely remote location, you will need a full trauma pack and someone trained to use it. You should seek advice on the most suitable course for your expedition, but a good start point is Expedition Medicine (see the list of Websites and Sources of Further Information). This runs excellent training courses focusing on the geographical areas of Jungle, Desert or Polar. Whatever type of trip you are going on, ensure you know what you will do if the worst should happen.

PREVENT

If you are travelling to a country where the medical facilities are limited or there are concerns about hygiene, then it is worth taking some additinal items.

Additional first-aid kit

- **sterile set** – *a sealed first-aid pack containing sterile needles, blades and materials that you can either use or give to a doctor to use instead of non-sterilised equipment – available from most outdoor shops; ensure it is sealed and stays in your hold baggage when travelling)*

- **dental set** – *allows you to fix a broken tooth with a temporary solution until you get to suitable dental attention*

- **sterile dressings** – *again to be used or given to a doctor without access to sterile equipment to prevent infection*

Sterile sets are available from travel shops and outlets.

Insurance issues

Many banks now offer travel insurance with their current accounts, or you can get annual travel insurance policies from almost anywhere, including the supermarket. Whichever policy you choose, the most important thing is to ensure it covers you for the activities you undertake. If you enjoy diving, free-fall parachuting or skiing off piste, pay the extra premium to get them on your policy. Take the original documents with you, as described on previous pages, but it is also worth leaving a copy with someone in the UK.

Do not be tempted to go without travel insurance. The costs of repatriation with a medical escort are incredibly high, and it is your responsibility to foot the bill. Even in Europe, while you can get treatment, it is your responsibility to fund your return trip. If you get a decent policy, it will also cover you for trips away from your home if you stay in the UK. It is worth noting that, if you get this wrong, the British Embassy will not pay for your return trip. The Embassy may in exceptional circumstances loan you some money for travel, but it is exactly that – a loan that will have robust repayment terms.

Leaving a travel plan

Whether you are going on a round-the-world trip or a week in the Med, it is always worth leaving a travel plan with a friend or relative. This can include details of how often you would like them to visit your house and also any important numbers and contacts, like your plumber or house insurance company. More importantly, you can leave emergency contact details for your hotel or travel agent and a date and time you are expecting to return. If you are travelling between locations, it is also sensible to leave an expected itinerary. Should anything untoward happen, at least the authorities have an idea of where you might be.

In addition to a travel plan, it is worth considering in detail how you will maintain contact with home. If your itinerary is changing or you decide to stay in one place for longer than expected, then remember to let people know. In some circumstances the very

It takes very little effort to stay in touch when you're away.

PREVENT

reason for a trip might be to get away from phone calls and emails, but you should agree your plans for communication before you go. Most mobile phones will work globally, and, if you really need to be in touch, satellite phones are becoming more affordable. Voice calls are expensive, but text messages tend to be significantly cheaper. For younger travellers on gap-year breaks there is the added pressure of keeping parents informed that all is well. Whether you like it or not, parents and family will worry about your safety, so a weekly email to your pals, copied to your parents, will ensure they have an idea that you are safe and in one piece.

Finally, if you really are going away for a long trip, do not underestimate the power of a letter or postcard. Anyone who has served overseas or been away for a long time will testify that an email is great, and a phone call is very enjoyable, but if you are missing home or really want to let someone know what a fantastic time you are having, there is nothing technology can do to replace a bit of paper that you've actually written on.

AIRPORTS AND OTHER ARRIVAL/DEPARTURE POINTS

Once you enter an airport or other international departure point, you need to be aware that the law may be different. With the increased tensions surrounding any potential terrorist attacks on international travel, it is worth remembering that a sense of humour has been surgically removed from most official security staff for very good reasons. DO NOT joke about bombs, terrorist incidents or the fact that someone else packed your bag in an airport; you could end up in jail.

Neither is being drunk in an airport particularly sensible. If your flights are delayed or there is a problem with your luggage, arguing with ground staff while intoxicated is likely to have a couple of simple effects: first, you won't be allowed on the aircraft and, secondly, you could end up in jail.

TERMINAL 1

① ② ③ ④

Traders selling items near departure points could be
offering more than you were bargaining for

Ensure your baggage is sealed before you check it in;
if necessary take a picture to prove its condition

In many instances, once you have cleared security, the
legal situation changes; be clear which country you are in

Do not get drunk in international arrival or
departure points

Remember all airports are monitored by CCTV; do not be
tempted to misbehave in an airport

⑥ *Keep your valuables close and do not get separated from your carry-on luggage*

⑦ *Children need close supervision in airports; consider whether they should look after their own passports*

⑧ *Your luggage will be handled by many people befor you see it again; make sure you check it when you collect it*

⑨ *Once on board and established, you can use the toil*

All places of entry or exit from a country are monitored by CCTV and many will routinely have covert surveillance officers keeping an eye on any unusual activity. If you undertake any kind of petty crime in an airport, you are asking for trouble, and the chances are you will end up in jail.

So a common theme! If you want to stay out of jail, behave when you are in an airport. It is also worth remembering that you may not be in the country you think you are. Those of you who have used the Channel Tunnel will know that there is a small bit of English soil in Kent that is actually legally France and therefore subject to French law, and that a little bit of earth near Calais is actually legally Blighty and is patrolled by British bobbies. This situation is not unique. When on board an aircraft you may be subject to international law, and abusive behaviour or refusal to extinguish a cigarette will carry hefty fines and in many cases prison sentences.

So, all international departure and arrival points have potentially more robust laws, increased surveillance and stiff penalties for non-compliance. Remain sober and aware of your surroundings, and most of all: behave!

Possible criminal activity

There is a simple truth about airports and other international arrival and departure points: criminals will be moving goods illegally through the same route as you. They will be looking for easy ways to do it and specifically for someone else to take the risk. You can avoid becoming involved very easily by following two simple rules:

- *never get separated from your baggage or kit when in or near an airport or other border crossing*

PREVENT

- never agree to carry anything or transport anything for anyone, at all, ever

The first rule is quite simple, but the second needs consideration. The chances are that 'Juan the drug smuggler' is not going to approach you in the airport lobby with a plastic bag full of heroin and ask you if you wouldn't mind delivering it to his brother at your destination. There are a number of scams you need to be aware of and counter:

You could be purchasing more than you bargained for at airports.

- ***Don't buy items from local traders in airports.*** *They can identify which flight you are booked on and may deliberately target you to sell you an item at an amazing price. Needless to say, the item you have bought will contain something that will be stolen to order from you at the other end. This may manifest itself as a violent robbery, so think whether you really do want to buy things at airports.*

- ***Ensure your baggage is properly secured before you check it in.*** *In a recent scandal in Australia baggage handlers used easily accessible luggage to transport drug packages to baggage handlers at another airport. In one case the 'receivers' missed the bag, and the allegedly unknowing mule is now spending life in an Indonesian jail. Lock your baggage using padlocks or similar, including the exterior pockets. If they are broken, you can point this out if you are stopped by customs.*

Secure your baggage. It will be handled by a lot of people before you see it again.

- ***Don't transport items across borders.*** *At international borders do not accept lifts or agree to drive someone else's vehicle. By the same token, never agree to deliver something to a friend or relative. Just say that you do not have the room in your bags.*

You may also be targeted for your money and/or travel documentation. Passports from Western countries carry a significant value, and criminals know to target weary travellers who are getting tired of dragging their luggage with them. Follow the guidance on carrying your documentation and keep your passport and money on your person **at all times.**

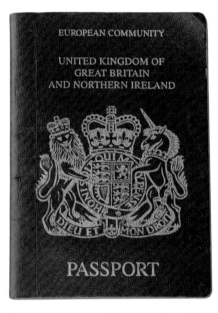

Your passport is a highly attractive item and you should keep it secure at all times.

Finally, you must be extremely vigilant when you are arriving at or leaving an airport or border area. Once you are outside the relative safety of the airside section of an airport or equivalent, you are exposed to the general population. You are quite easy to identify and you are likely to be carrying a passport, MP3 player, mobile phone, credit and debit cards and, most importantly, cash. You are unlikely to know how much anything costs on arrival, and could be extremely tired and therefore less aware. All this means airports offer great pickings for criminals. If possible, always arrange to be met from an airport by someone you can recognise. If you can't do this, always use the authorised taxi rank and agree a price before you get in the cab. Whatever you do, keep your belongings with you at all times and focus on leaving the airport as quickly as possible.

Carrying your belongings

When arriving at or leaving an airport or border crossing, it is particularly important that you carry your belongings in a way that allows you best to protect yourself and to move freely. This is a good idea for many reasons, not least because none of us enjoys heaving heavy suitcases around crowded airports.

PREVENT

Hold baggage

If you know you are going to have a lot of baggage, consider before you travel whether the old suitcase without wheels and a slightly dodgy zip is the best idea, or if the peace of mind and ease of a newer, solid bag with wheels might be well worth the cost. There are a hundred and one types of bag or rucksack, and to recommend one over another would be ridiculous. Choose something that best allows you to move freely. For me this normally means a large robust holdall that has rucksack-type straps that I can clip off at check-in and clip on at the baggage collection point. I can then carry all my kit on my back and move quickly with my hands free. For my wife it is a stiff-based large holdall with wheels for getting through the airport and then a set

Think carefully about your hold baggage and most of all ensure you can secure it shut.

of rucksack straps so it can be carried easily over rough ground. For my mother it is a solid suitcase with wheels and a comfortable handle. If you are going on a gap year or travelling between locations, then some kind of rucksack may be the best choice. Ensure that you can secure it effectively, including all the pockets, once you get to check-in. You may find that putting your rucksack in a linen bag with a secured opening is a useful way of keeping all the straps away from the baggage handling mechanisms and ensuring no one has put anything in its pockets. Once it comes off the baggage carousel, you can take it out of the linen sack and re-shoulder it.

Hand luggage

If possible, choose an item of hand luggage that has a shoulder strap so you can carry it with your hands free. This prevents you having to put it down every time you are asked to produce your tickets or pay for a drink. Much as we discussed in connection with carrying your bag in the street, the best place for a bag is not slung over your shoulder but by your side, so it is still in your peripheral vision. Keep your essential documents and any medications in your hand luggage.

About your person

If I'm travelling in a temperate climate, I often carry a waterproof jacket with zipped pockets containing all my bits and bobs. That way I know I have my passport, wallet and any other important items about my person and secured. If you are travelling in a warmer climate, consider wearing a pair of loose trousers with zip or button-close pockets. You can then ensure your important items are secure. Particularly useful are trousers with a sealable 'map pocket' on the leg. This can be used to keep passport, tickets and boarding pass to hand.

Before you arrive at the departure point, fit your concealed wallet and ensure it is comfortable. Do not use it for your passport or items you will need. It defeats the point when you have to reveal your concealed wallet at check-in, and then at the departures gate, and then at security . . . If you want something to hand rather than a pocket, use a bum-bag for your passport and other travel documentation.

Once you are on the aircraft, train or ship, keep all your items in your pockets, your concealed belt hidden and your bum-bag on. If you have a jacket, place it in your footwell. Wait until the aircraft has taken off and everyone is settled and then use a trip to the toilet to get comfortable and privately remove your concealed

PREVENT

money belt and other items. I take off my money belt, remove my wallet, passport and documents out of my pockets and secure them inside my wash bag or zipped filofax. I then keep everything in the seat pocket in front of me, where I can keep an eye on it, and grab it quickly if required. I am comfortable on the journey and can hold it in my lap when sleeping.

Carrying a newspaper or magazine on a journey fills time and allows you to scribble notes.

Once the aircraft is coming into my destination, I reverse the process and use the visit to the toilet to freshen up and ensure I am alert. I can refamiliarise myself about either who is meeting me or which hire car company I need to find.

This can all seem a little extreme, but, aside from being good sense, it gives you something to think about on a journey, breaks the journey down into separate phases and helps pass the time. Apart from the security implications, there are also good reasons to have all your kit to hand and be alert when landing or taking off. If the worst should ever occur and you are asked to evacuate the aircraft, you know that you have everything to hand and can concentrate on making your escape.

Finally, consider carrying a newspaper or magazine when you travel. I scribble my departure times and information on it, so I can refer to them without having to get my tickets out. It gives me something to read and provides an excellent excuse not to speak to people if I'm sitting on my own.

Offers of help and assistance

Most people are inherently polite and if engaged in conversation will reply. Most of us feel a little rude if we do not show interest in a fellow human being or feel compassion for someone having a bad time. But you should be extremely careful when in airports or around border crossings if people engage you in conversation or ask for assistance. By the same virtue, be overtly cautious of people offering you a lift or volunteering to carry your bags when you arrive in an airport. It is a sad reflection of the modern world, but you really are better off being robust, even if you feel you are being rude. Remain self-interested and steer away from conversation with strangers while in airports or border crossings. An easy strategy is to be polite but disinterested if someone engages you in conversation. Again, I find that having a newspaper or magazine to hand and continuing to read it if someone speaks sends the right message without being too rude.

TRANSPORT: TAXIS AND HIRE CARS

When you are abroad, you will no doubt need to travel and, unless you hire a car, you will be sharing your environment. In order to avoid becoming a victim of a crime, it is worth considering some common crime scenarios and how to avoid them.

Hire cars

Many hire cars carry clearly defined markings; in fact in some countries they have different number plates. This is unfortunate, as anything that identifies a car as being a tourist vehicle is likely to attract criminals. If you can, and it's not going to wreck the car, remove anything that immediately identifies it as holding potential pickings. In most countries, this is now limited to a

PREVENT

sticker in the rear window or on the bumper. I always remove these and have yet to be challenged when I return it. In resorts where there is a specific tourist car (for example, a Mini Moke or Jeep), consider whether you really want one of these, or whether a small car with air conditioning might actually be safer and more appropriate.

Taxis

There are different traditions and local customs for taxis all over the world. By reading your travel guide before you arrive, you will hopefully have an idea about whether it is normal to tip a driver and how much you should expect to pay. Always get a taxi from a recognised rank or call a company; where possible avoid bartering on the streets. The golden rule, even in developed countries with taxis on a meter, is to agree a price before either you or your bags

Agree a price before you get into a taxi, whether at home or abroad.

get into the cab. Even in London, taxi drivers will give you a rough price if you ask. Most altercations involving taxis are about the bill. These can be completely avoided by agreeing a price at the start and keeping an eye on the route being used.

Language is, of course, always a challenge, but the conversation to aim for is something like 'Hello, I'd like to get to the city hotel in Brown Street, please, by the most direct route; the information desk told me it should cost around 20 dollars'. If I'm able to communicate, I often ask the taxi driver to talk me through

the sights on the route on my map as we go. Asking about the local places of interest and what road we're on at the moment means it's incredibly difficult to be taken on a round-the-houses trip if you really are from out of town. Ensure your doors are locked if you are in a location that may be subject to muggings and also that your luggage is either locked in a boot or in the cab with you. Avoid travelling with your bags in the back of a pick-up truck or somewhere where they can be grabbed.

Hitch-hiking

The simple rule on hitch-hiking is don't do it. Many people have romantic memories of the days when you could safely hitch-hike round the UK without fear of being attacked. I'm afraid they are just that – romantic memories. Hitch-hiking in the UK has been a high-risk activity for some time and we are a relatively crime-free country. If you hitch-hike, you are asking for trouble. By the same token, do not pick up hitch-hikers and also be wary about when and where to stop. The faked car crash is used in many countries to lure tourists into a carjacking scenario. Ensure you are well read up on possible threats in the country you are visiting.

There are still people who hitch-hike, but it remains a very high-risk activity.

Public transport

Public transport in many countries is not as reliable or as regulated as it is in the UK. For example, what to you might look like a public bus service may be a private one, used only by locals, where the driver can charge what he wants and you are certainly

PREVENT

not welcome. The best thing to do is ask at your hotel reception, a tourist information centre, or talk to a friendly barman, before you try to use a public transport system. They will also be able to tell you what you need to be aware of – for example, I would tell anyone using the London Tube for the first time to be wary of pickpockets.

In simple terms the same advice applies to foreign transport as it does to using public transport in the UK (see Chapter 5). Choose where you want to sit, conduct a 5 and 20 check, and, if you feel uncomfortable, do something about it. Either move or get off.

Check before you use a bus service abroad.

HOTELS AND ACCOMMODATION

The first thing to consider is which hotel to choose. In many instances you are going to leave your most valued possessions with the reception team. You will probably give them your credit-card details and, while you are out for the day, you are going to trust them with your belongings and a key to your room. Choosing between a ropey hotel and spending £10 a night more to get somewhere you feel happy with should be an easy decision. If your hotel gives you an electronic card key, be aware that this will carry more information than you think. It will probably electronically hold

You are going to want to use your hotel reception for advice and possibly to store valuables. It is worth choosing a reliable and safe place to stay.

HOTEL

1
2
3
4
5
6

FIRE

194

In hot countries, balconies and windows are favourite entry points; if you can, get a room with air conditioning ①

All hotels are insecure; consider your room door as a door to the outside world ②

Only use your room safe for items you are happy to replace or have insured; room safes are notoriously insecure ③

Your key card contains more information than you think; keep it safe ④

The hotel safe is more secure than one in your room, but make sure you always get a receipt; if necessary, photograph your belongings ⑤

Your first action when you reach your room should always be to check the location of the fire escapes ⑥

your name, home address, credit-card details and room number. So, if you lose it, theoretically a criminal could steal everything from your room, empty your credit card and phone his mate in the UK to inform him that your home is empty and ripe for burglary! Keep electronic room cards safe and secure at all times.

When you arrive in a hotel room, it is sensible and safety conscious to walk the fire escape with whoever you are staying with. This should include opening the doors out of the building or, if they appear alarmed, at least asking to ensure they are not locked. At the same time, see if it is possible to open the windows of the room or interlinking doors. This is not only useful for fire safety; you will also find out how accessible your room is to non-residents.

Your card key has more information on it than you think; keep it safe.

Where to leave your valuables

This is an age-old problem that comes down to judgement. Most hotels have a 'secure' facility for you to put your valuables in. Many hotels also provide a room safe. It is almost always more secure to use the hotel reception safe, where you can get a receipt, rather than rely on a room facility. A useful precaution is to use your camera or phone to photograph what you are handing over to reception to be put into the safe. In some instances, if you are in the developing world or forced to stay in what you might feel is a particularly untrustworthy hotel, you may be better off

PREVENT

either keeping your valuables on your person or securing them in your room. It comes down to your own risk assessment, but I have previously found myself in a position where I felt the most sensible option was to keep some money on me, put some in the hotel safe and hide the rest behind the shower panel in my room – the logic being I would have to be very unlucky to get mugged, robbed and have the hotel 'lose' my money! The easiest solution is to ensure you don't take many valuables with you when you travel.

Securing your room

When you are out of the room, you should consider it completely insecure, even in modern Western countries. Even the finest hotels can find themselves the victims of unscrupulous house staff. Do not leave anything of value in your room unless it is hidden or secured in a suitable location and you are prepared to accept the risk. When you are in your room, you should always use the manual door lock. With the right appearance and confidence you can wander around the corridors of even the most exclusive hotels without being challenged. Criminals know this, so you should treat your hotel door as a door to the street and keep it locked. There is normally a chain or door bar; use it when you answer the door. If you are in a warm climate and your hotel room has a balcony and sliding doors, you need to consider the risk from people coming through the open balcony doors – both during the day, when the room is vacant, and at night-time, while you are in your bed. The safest option is to find a room with air conditioning and keep the doors and windows shut. If you have to sleep in an unsecured room, then stack things in your favour by making it difficult to get in quietly and ensuring you have something to hand to use as a weapon should you be woken in the night.

Remember, there is more than one way to get into your hotel room.

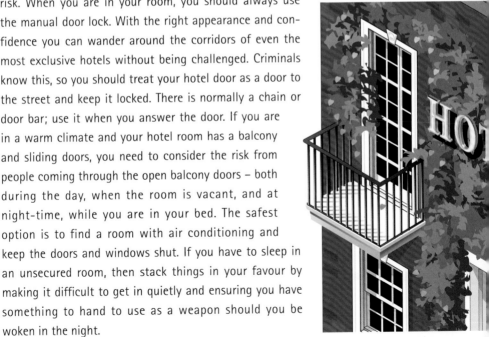

Passports and other documents

Remember, once you are established in your accommodation, the best solution is to put your passport and key original documents in the hotel safe. Carry a photocopy with you while you are out and have a sealed envelope secreted somewhere in your luggage with copies of everything.

STRATEGIES TO AVOID IDENTIFYING YOURSELF AS A VICTIM

If you live in an area frequented by tourists, you will no doubt be able to pick many of them out of the crowd by their appearance and actions. They might dress differently, speak differently or be festooned with cameras and guidebooks. We have already discussed options for dress and carrying kit, but it is worth considering some specific activities that will identify you as a potential victim. The chances are that, whatever you do, you are going to stick out as a non-local, particularly in developing countries. Criminals will guess that you are carrying a camera, a mobile phone and other electrical goods, significant sums of cash and more usefully a Western passport. There are some simple steps you can take to tone down your appearance as someone from out of town, without resorting to purchasing a false moustache and glasses. The trick is to accept that you don't look like a local and to give the appearance of someone who is comfortable in his or her environment.

The most common items that identify you as a tourist are a map, guidebook and camera. The rules for carrying these items are quite simple. A camera, whether in your home country or abroad, should never be carried outside your clothing and around your neck. It acts as an advertisement to any criminal, immediately identifies you as someone from out of town, and provides a handy strap for an assailant to injure you with. Keep your camera in a

PREVENT

bag or pocket and produce it only when you want to take a picture. This is good advice if for no other reason than it helps to protect your camera from damage.

Maps and guidebooks should be small and kept tidy, and you should prepare them in your hotel room before you go out for the day. Fully unfolding your 1-metre-square tourist guide on a street corner in any city in the world is akin to holding up a sign that says: 'I'm new here and don't know where I am. Please rob me.' A simple strategy, and one that is widely used, is to buy a local language magazine or newspaper and slide your map or tourist guide into the pages. This allows you to keep your street guide tucked under one arm for regular reference while also giving the initial impression that you are either of local origin or can speak the language and are familiar with the area.

Apart from the items you carry, the way you dress may also be different from the locals and identify you as a tourist. We have covered this before, but it is worth considering what you will wear, because I hope you now agree that branded, expensive-looking or

Carrying your city guide in a local language magazine means you can keep it to hand and read a bit about the local culture without being too obvious.

clearly Western clothing does not make great travel gear. If you look at professional travelling clothing produced by companies like Rohan, you will see products that are plain and functional, but certainly not dull or unfashionable.

The same points are even more relevant to your choice of jewellery. If you own an expensive branded watch, the chances are that it looks like an expensive branded watch. Wearing all your finest gold is also probably not a sensible option. It might also be the case that wearing all your cheapest jewellery is not the best course of action either. Consider this: if you identify yourself as a decadent tourist by carrying your camera around your neck and wearing your brand new trainers, is a developing-world thief going to think your cheap diamante costume jewellery is real or fake? He'll probably only worry about it once he has it safely in his possession.

When abroad, try to dress in practical, comfortable and non-branded clothing.

Activities to avoid

The main rule to follow to ensure you don't end up in a jail cell is to avoid anything that is against the law or could be seen as being against the law. This is not as obvious as it sounds. It does not only mean staying away from drugs or the sex industry; it also means steering clear of any demonstrations or large public gatherings. In many countries the authorities do not respond well to public criticism, and joining what may appear to you to be a low-key protest – for example, against human-rights violations or child slavery – may end up with you being jailed for a significant period of time. Whatever your personal beliefs, consider very carefully the implications of becoming involved with pressure groups in other countries. Even an association with a known

PREVENT

activist may be enough for you to be identified as a potential threat to national security.

If you haven't found out before you go, when you arrive ensure you get to know if there are any less welcoming parts of town and stay away from them. If you think about your own town or city, you can probably think of an area you wouldn't send a tourist to. There's an equivalent spot in almost every town in the world: make sure you know where it is.

Depending on the country you are in and whether you are in an area frequented by tourists, it may also be worth thinking about the bars and restaurants and which ones are clearly tourist hot spots. Most tourist destinations by definition have three general areas – the tourists' bit, the locals' bit and an area where the two blur slightly. In many places the tourist bars are deliberately targeted by pickpockets and other traders, and you will undoubtedly find the prices are inflated to take account of your wealth. Tourists may not be welcome in the locals' area, but certainly the prices will be lower and the experience will be of the real culture. The areas on the fringe generally offer a more authentic local experience and a better blend of locals and tourists. The prices also tend to be a bit more reasonable.

While the tourist areas of town will cater for your every need, they will probably also be targeted by criminals.

Wherever you decide to eat or drink in the evenings, it is also worth considering the 'allegiance' of any location. I can think of tourist locations where it is clear that there is a German bar, a British bar and an American bar. Make sure you keep track of the political situation and what's happening in the news; it might just be that drinking in the American or British bar is not the most sensible option. Drinking elsewhere not only mitigates the risk of being involved in a terrorist attack, but also avoids the far more likely problems of aggravation or theft. Sometimes the best protection may be to stay away from other tourists altogether.

Think about the profile of the places you eat and drink.

IF YOU ARE A VICTIM

Violent crime is violent crime the world over. There is little difference on the surface between someone who will attack you for your wallet in Birmingham because he needs his next fix of heroin and a street mugger in a developing country. There is, however, a difference that you should always bear in mind if you find yourself in a violent-crime situation while travelling. You can just about guarantee that the criminal in the developing world will place a different value on life than you do and will certainly be prepared to escalate the level of violence very rapidly if you decide you want to fight. (This, of course, can be true in the UK, but the UK criminal is often conducting a cost–risk–benefit analysis that you can influence with your actions.) If you bear this in mind, it is almost always the case that handing over a wallet or valuable item is, in the long term, the safest option. There are, of course, situations where it may be appropriate that you defend yourself, and you should use the advice given in Chapter 8 tempered with an understanding that someone armed with a knife or gun may be entirely willing to use it.

If you have been robbed or attacked, report it to the police and if appropriate to the British Embassy or Consulate. This not only ensures that the necessary follow-up action can be taken, but also means you will have a crime number for your insurance company.

PREVENT

CHAPTER SEVEN

Global Terrorism

I f you are travelling to a tourist resort in a first-world city or country, then the advice contained in Chapter 5 is most relevant for you – the types of threat in Western Europe are similar to those in countries like the USA or Australia.

If you are travelling to somewhere other than a first-world city, it is worth considering the wider threats that country may pose. In many cases tourist resorts frequented by British and Western tourists deliberately have the look and feel of the West, but are actually relatively false oases in countries that are very different from ours. These resorts are often in countries that are suffering from internal struggles or are victims of international terrorism. The local population may be actively anti-West, and the resort you are staying in may be seen as a soft target. In these instances the general information in Chapter 6 about how to stay safe when travelling abroad will provide you with a good understanding of what to avoid and how to behave, but there are some specific things to be aware of.

If you are truly travelling to a location not normally frequented by tourists, then you should consider how it might differ from other places you have visited in terms of threat, so you can adjust your responses accordingly.

If you're working here, then you need to take more than a passing interest in your security.

This chapter focuses on general advice for people who are travelling with tour operators or on the relatively well-beaten track. It does not include the special information required by those who are going to countries where Westerners are actively targeted by terrorist organisations. If you are travelling, for pleasure or business, to a country where you may be targeted – for example, Iraq, Afghanistan or some African countries – then your security needs to become more than a passing interest and you should be signing up for a hostile environment course and confirming details of your protection while you are in the country.

This chapter will not cover subjects such as mine awareness, kidnap and rescue protocols, or what to carry in your pockets if you are working in a hostile environment. While the demands of

PREVENT

the modern business world mean that a significant number of British and Western people need to know these skills, they are specialist subjects and will not be discussed here.

Even in some of the better-frequented tourist resorts, you should be aware that, on their own ground, terrorists may be more willing to take risks and openly target Westerners. In some parts of the world it may also be the norm for rebels to fight open gun battles within earshot of where you are staying. It is worth finding this out before you go! The Foreign & Commonwealth Office website (see the list of Websites and Sources of Further Information) is the best source of up-to-date information.

TYPES OF ATTACK

In a foreign country the range of methods available to terrorists is the same as in the UK. All that may change is the terrorists' ability to operate more freely and the level of risk they are prepared to accept. All the attack methods covered below could also occur in the West, but it is worth considering their particular implications when you travel further afield.

Suicide bomb

Despite the attacks of 7/7, people in the UK have not been subjected to a long-term suicide bombing campaign. Many countries that have had to deal with this threat for some time will have measures in place to defend against it. It does not mean the place is necessarily any more dangerous than your home country, but you should be aware of the protocols. If you visit Tel Aviv and go to a restaurant or bar, the doormen might be armed and might carry out airport-style searches as you go in. You might also notice that the entrance areas are normally far more robust than in the UK and have actually been reinforced to ensure that, if someone is

1. *If you want to remain aware of what's going on, sit outside or find a spot near the entrance with your back to something solid*

2. *If you are driving what is clearly a tourist vehicle in a high-threat area, ensure you search it regularly*

3. *In times of increased tension, it may be safer to avoid the 'tourist' bars*

4. *Expect to see heavily armed security in resorts where there is a threat of attack; and remember, if you misbehave, it's the man with the shotgun who will come to remove you*

5. *Suicide bombers are not easy to spot or defeat; if you are suspicious of someone with a bag or bulky clothing, have the confidence to act to prevent your involvement*

6. *A truck bomb will cause devastation to lightweight structures; be alert for suspicious vehicles*

caught entering the premises carrying a device, people inside are not injured.

It is not possible to draw a profile of what a suicide bomber looks like, so trying to spot one is a task doomed to failure. Similarly, it is difficult to act in a way that defends against them, because they attack without warning.

Remember that a carried device by its very nature will be small and will probably be lethal over only a small area. If you suspect something is about to happen, try to get distance between you and the bomber, and if possible get something solid between you and the device.

Consider what kind of location might be attacked by a suicide bomber. Restaurants or bars that routinely serve Westerners are high on the list of places that have been attacked. When you eat or drink in a place that might be targeted, if possible sit somewhere where you can see the entrance or somewhere relatively protected like an alcove. Alternatively, sitting outdoors means that you will avoid the effects of any blast that may be contained by the building and also allows you to move quickly away from any possible threat. If there are formal warnings in your resort that an attack is expected, it is worth considering eating and drinking in locations that you know have decent security. If you can eat by the side of the pool in a hotel with secure grounds and access control, perhaps that is the most sensible thing to do rather than trying to sample the local experience downtown.

Car bomb

In some tourist locations you may be told that you could be at risk from a car bomb. This is an extremely grave threat, as it represents a risk of death, so it is worth taking it seriously if it is mentioned. There are a number of ways of placing a car bomb and therefore only a full search can truly eliminate the threat. However, it is good practice to carry out a visual check of the bottom of your car

PREVENT

An under-vehicle car bomb is a relatively simple and widely used device.

if you think you may be at risk. The most simple way is to look under the driver's seat, which is the most likely location for a device to be placed. In order to do this you first need to know what the area under your driver's seat normally looks like to know if there is anything untoward. So when you are given a hire car, have a good look at the underside to see what bumps and lumps are normal.

The easiest way to carry out such a search is to walk to the driver's side door and, without placing any weight against the car, crouch onto one knee and have a good look under the vehicle. If you feel self-conscious doing this, disguise your activity by dropping your car keys as you approach your vehicle and have a good look as you stoop to pick them up.

If your vehicle is left outside at night-time, then you may wish to carry out a more thorough search in the mornings. This should include the underside of your car, the wheel arches and the engine bay. A good tool to help with this is a mirror on a stick. You may be able to buy one with a torch attached; otherwise you can improvise by using a make-up mirror to help in your search.

Weapons of mass destruction

The chances of a chemical, biological, radiological or nuclear attack in an area where small arms and explosives are freely available is in most cases lower than it is in a modern Western city. Moreover, in all instances, it is far more likely that a terrorist will employ a tactic known to be successful – for example, a bomb or an arson attack – than something highly complex that is at risk of failure. If you do believe that a non-conventional attack is under way, head upwind and away from the site of the attack as quickly as possible.

PREVENT

Acts of war

In many countries the war on terror is open conflict that represents the norm, and the terrorists are not shadowy figures who plot and bomb. They are organised units who may have been in disagreement with the authorities for decades. In such countries, it is expected that the political opposition will have a military wing that may have to operate using methods more akin to terrorism. It is worth remembering that one man's terrorist is another man's freedom fighter and that a good way to attract attention in the media is to target Westerners. At the end of 2006 there were eight major wars under way on the planet (defined by the UN as conflict where there are more than a 1,000 battlefield deaths every year) and about twenty-three 'lesser' conflicts of varying intensity. If you take into account that, as a whole, around 75 per cent of the casualties of all conflicts since the millennium have been non-combatants, it is entirely possible if you travel widely that at some point you may experience a firefight or be exposed to shelling or other acts of war.

If you become involved in a firefight, take cover and stay there. This means finding something solid to hide behind, or, if you can't find anything suitable, getting on the floor and making yourself as small as possible. Try not to present yourself as a target, so certainly don't pick up a weapon or take any other action that could identify you as a combatant. Once the immediate firing is over, you should leave the area as quickly as possible, particularly if there has been shelling; this can often be a precursor to an attack.

Arms are widely available in the developing world and in many countries the AK47 is a standard item of everyday equipment. Travel widely enough and you will eventually be in the wrong place at the wrong time.

SENSIBLE ACTIONS TO TAKE TO AVOID BEING INVOLVED

As in avoiding crime in a foreign country, it helps not to identify yourself openly as a decadent tourist from the West with stereotypical views. Loudly discussing the merits of the current operations in Iraq using phrases like 'we opened a can of whoop ass!' is unlikely to endear you to your fellow tourists, let alone the locals. Apart from following the general advice about not standing out, you should also ensure that you are culturally aware and not causing offence to local people. Check you know any local customs or sensitivities before you travel.

Walking around like this in many places in the world will attract all the wrong sorts of attention.

PREVENT

Watch the locals

The way local people behave is an excellent barometer for the amount of tension in an area, or an indication if something is about to go wrong. Sometimes local people will know if an attack is going to happen. So, if the streets are bizarrely empty, it may be worth leaving the area. At the simplest level, the locals will spot someone 'dodgy' far more quickly than you will, and will react. If they are leaving or acting in an agitated manner, you need to become alert and try to see what they have seen.

World events

Even if you are immersing yourself in the experience of being on holiday and have no mobile phone or laptop, it is worth keeping one eye on world events. Terrorists often attack in retaliation for events that happen on a global scale. So, if there has been a particularly controversial incident in Iraq, Afghanistan or the Middle East, there may be increased tensions between the tourists and the locals in those areas and elsewhere. By the same token, local political actions can lead to tensions. Some holiday resorts are not happy places around election time, or if a violent political drama is unfolding.

During times of increased tension, it will pay you to ensure that you avoid places where any threat is more likely to manifest itself. Bars or restaurants that are known as expat or Western spots may be targeted. You should also avoid political gatherings and demonstrations, and, if things are very sensitive, you should think carefully about avoiding all large public gatherings such as sporting events, or even tourist attractions.

Whatever the situation, never get separated from your kit. If you are travelling or working in an area where a terrorist attack is a possibility, then it is prudent to ensure that you always have some essentials with you, such as a passport (or copy), your wallet and some cash, your insurance documents and perhaps a small first-aid kit. In this kind of situation it is sensible for a number of reasons to keep your bags close to hand, so consider using a small shoulder bag that you can carry comfortably.

WHAT TO DO IN THE IMMEDIATE AFTERMATH

Immediately after an attack, your priority must be to find yourself a place of safety. Unless you are directly involved and therefore at the site offering first-aid assistance, you need to consider that quite often an attack is followed up with another similar incident at a location close by or with other violent action. So get away from the immediate area and get yourself to somewhere you know to be safe. That may not be the hotel where you are staying, but could be a place you have visited or a restaurant you know.

Do not expect fantastic medical facilities if you are overseas. Often you may be better served by getting patched up and sent home.

Medical facilities

If you are injured or in need of medical attention, you need to conduct a conscious risk assessment of the seriousness of the problem and the medical treatment you are likely to receive. You

may be staying in a smart resort, but that doesn't necessarily mean that the hospital serving the area is modern and well supported. If you have a minor injury and you know that hospital facilities are basic or perhaps likely to be treating locals with a high incidence of HIV, perhaps you would

PREVENT

be better to choose to tidy up your cuts using your own first-aid pack. You may not have the luxury of making this decision, but, if you can take control yourself, do so.

Organise

Once the dust has settled, you need to organise quickly. Account for everyone in your group and then return to wherever your belongings are and start to pull things together so that you are prepared to move at short notice. It is always sensible to establish a rendezvous point in a resort for family or friends in case one of you gets lost or separated – a location near to but not actually in your hotel is a sensible choice. By establishing this at the start of your holiday, you can ensure everyone has a simple way of getting together in all eventualities.

Inform

There are a number of groups who will be concerned about you in the aftermath of a major incident. First and most importantly, ensure your immediate group and, if you have one, your tour

Rolling media coverage has to be interesting and is often sensational. If you are involved in an incident, try to let your loved ones know that you are safe as soon as possible.

operator are aware that you are safe. This includes letting your hotel know you are all right and back in the building. Secondly, the British Embassy will swing into action very quickly after a major incident and in some smaller resorts will know which individuals are probably in the area. Letting the Embassy know you are safe and well will prevent it wasting resources on trying to find you. Finally, the global media machine will take minutes to report any major incident in a tourist location and the initial coverage is often confusing and sensational. If you can get a call or email through to someone at home, do so, and ask that person to call all your friends and family to let them know you are safe. This saves you wasting valuable time on the phone.

Evacuate

Sometimes people have a strong desire to remain in a location in the immediate aftermath of a major incident. However, the best advice is always to evacuate the area as quickly and efficiently as is practical. If it is not possible for you to change your return flights, consider finding alternative accommodation in other resorts in the same country.

SUPPORT FROM THE EMBASSY OR HIGH COMMISSION

The Embassy or High Commission in each country has a number of roles to fulfil, only one of them being to support UK nationals in the area. If you are in a particularly remote or dangerous location, it is only polite to try to make their job easier. If you arrive in a terrorist hot spot, there may be arrangements for UK citizens to book into the Embassy and then book out on departure. Ensure you do book out – not doing so can cause major problems for busy staff.

PREVENT

If there has been a major incident or catastrophe, the Foreign & Commonwealth Office may decide to offer exceptional assistance above and beyond what is normally provided. The nature of the incident will determine the level of help that is deemed appropriate. In general terms, this may extend to actions such as:

- *medical evacuation to a place of safety (not necessarily the UK)*

- *transportation of bodies or remains to the UK*

- *travel for members of the family to the location of an attack*

While the Embassy or High Commission will try to help, do not expect them to organise your medical repatriation. Make sure you are insured.

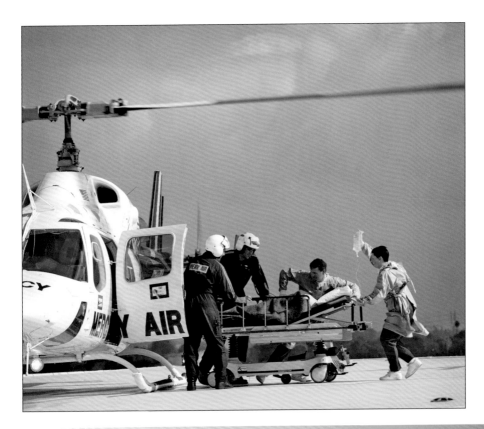

If you have been involved in a catastrophic event, the FCO may also arrange for you to be debriefed when you return to the UK and be provided with aftercare.

In all circumstances it is generally assumed that you are responsible for your own actions. This means that the FCO will expect you to have checked its website before travel. If it has advised against travel to a particular country and you have gone anyway, quite rightly it may be less than enthusiastic to spend significant amounts of taxpayers' money on assisting you. It will also expect you to have adequate travel and medical insurance. There is no requirement for the FCO to pay your medical bills or help with the cost of repatriation. In summary, in extreme circumstances the FCO can swing into action very quickly to assist you; it has well-established plans for the evacuation of UK Entitled Persons from just about any situation, if necessary with assistance from the MOD. However, do not expect the FCO to bail you out if you have ignored its advice or been reckless.

PREVENT

CHAPTER EIGHT

Self-Defence

The best form of self-defence is the avoidance of situations where violence may occur. This approach guarantees your safety. So, if you follow the advice given in this book, you will hopefully never find yourself in a situation where you need to **PROTECT** and defend yourself; you will have taken steps to PRE-EMPT any violent situation and PREVENT your involvement.

Physical intervention should always be the last resort. However, if a situation escalates to the point where you are required to use force, the advice from the majority of people who comment on these issues is to use as much force as is required to remove the threat to your safety, and then to leave the area as quickly as possible. In short, hit and run. This technique might seem overly simple, but it is taught consistently to members of the police and military who might be required to look after themselves.

There are many providers of self-defence training in the UK. They fall into two broad groups – conflict resolution and martial arts. Confusingly this means that there is more than one governing body for the delivery of self-defence training in the UK. Use common sense if you are looking for a course provider and ask to speak to someone who has done the course before. Unless you are

Do not be afraid to run away – it is often the best form of defence.

motivated to learn martial arts or complex self-defence techniques, keep everything as simple as possible. Practising with your partner or a friend can help you to visualise what you might do, but ensure you don't actually hurt each other! It is very easy to get carried away when learning these skills, so deliberately choose someone sensible to practise with.

THE REALITIES OF VIOLENCE

There are no rules when a situation between two people degenerates into violence. There are, however, some simple truths.

It is very rare for any party to walk away from a physical confrontation uninjured. If you decide to use violence, you can expect to get injured in the process.

Unless you have spent a significant amount of your life learning self-defence or martial arts, and even if you have, the truth is that the stronger person is likely to come out on top. If you are not the

PROTECT

stronger person, you need to rely heavily on surprise and quick decisive action.

Defending yourself doesn't have to be fair. Judges will not ask if you boxed according to Queensbury rules while defending yourself, and criminals have no approved code of conduct. If you have made the decision that you need to apply violence to protect yourself, then don't mess about.

Criminals do not follow an approved code of conduct or box to Queensbury rules. As long as you act to defend yourself, the law will protect you.

The law will be on your side if you act to protect yourself and use reasonable force. However, if you injure someone who no longer poses a threat, quite rightly you will find yourself on the wrong side of the law. If a situation arises where you need to use violence, you should be confident about your legal position. So read your rights in detail before the situation occurs. You will find a link on the police website, which is included in the list of Websites and Sources of Further Information.

Self-Defence

The best self-defence is not to get involved in a violent incident to start with. Initially, we will consider how to turn an escalating situation into a non-event.

De-escalate

If you believe that a situation may be moving towards a violent resolution, the first thing to try is to calm the situation and talk your way out. Try to defuse any situation initially by being non-threatening. If someone wants your money, explain that you don't want to get hurt and you will give them the money you have but you don't have very much – perhaps they would do better asking someone else. If you are female and confronted by someone in a sexually predatory manner, try to humanise yourself in the potential attacker's mind. You could indicate that you are unwell or that you need to get home to a child. Do anything you can to make the attacker think of you as a human being or someone not worth the bother rather than as a victim. While talking, try to keep some distance between yourself and the potential attacker and mentally prepare yourself for a rapid escalation to violence. Turning your body sideways can present a less threatening image; you should also ensure you are well balanced in case you are pushed. Sitting down can cool people's tempers, so in a pub or club, when confronted by aggression, think about whether it is appropriate and possible to sit down and talk.

Keep talking

If the situation continues to build but doesn't escalate rapidly, follow some simple rules about your verbal and non-verbal communication. The aim is always to keep the option open for the

PROTECT

situation to defuse or for you to get away, while maintaining your assertiveness. Look for the opportunity to break contact with the person, but do not simply turn your back mid-conversation. If someone is still talking, the chances are he or she is still forming a decision as to whether to attack you or not. Your body language should be positive and assertive to demonstrate that you are not prepared to become a victim. Do not raise your voice or use pointing or jabbing motions; use slow steady hand movements and maintain eye contact but avoid frowning or glaring. Try to keep your voice calm but deliberate (even though you will probably feel anything but). If you can, speak with confidence and use phrases like:

In a situation of heightened emotion, your body language says more than you think.

- 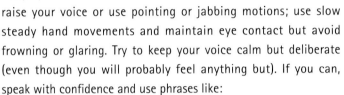 *'You will **not** get my phone.'*

- *'**Don't** do that to me.'*

- *' I want you to leave my property **now**.'*

- *'I do **not** want to have sex with you.'*

Use this time to plan. Do not allow yourself to become animated or overcome with emotion. Your best asset is your brain, so stay calm and give yourself the time to come up with options.

Distract

If it becomes clear that conversation will not resolve the situation and you need to break off, try a simple distraction technique. This may sound childish, but it can work if all you need is a moment to make your escape. If you are the victim of a robbery in a reasonably public place, then consider dropping whatever it is you have been asked for on the floor. As you take your wallet out and open it up, drop some notes on the floor in front of your attacker; if he or she stoops, you can either attack or run. Pointing over someone's shoulder and shouting for imaginary assistance is not going to get you any more than a second of time, but if that's what you need why not try it? Finally, there are situations where faking a panic attack, or a more serious problem, may completely unhinge a potential attacker. This can certainly be useful if there are other people around you – for example, in a bar – who may then morally feel you deserve some help.

BASIC SELF-DEFENCE: VIOLENCE

There are many books, courses and martial-arts disciplines that will teach you ad infinitum how to react to every possible self-defence situation. If you have time to learn one of these disciplines, it can be a very rewarding hobby that will of course give you some valuable experience and skills. If you do study self-defence, you must recognise that the violence that occurs on our streets is different from what you encounter in a class environment and it is important that you maintain a realistic view. Below are some general considerations about violence.

It is interesting that unarmed combat taught to soldiers who may need to fight for their lives bears little resemblance to pure martial arts. More importantly, it is far more brutal than the litigiously minded techniques taught on police and public self-defence courses. Never let a qualification in some form of physical defence technique cloud your decision making – a truly deter-mined attacker is unlikely to start in the ready position, or allow you a second chance at the arm grab you've been practising. If you enter a physical engagement, the likelihood is you will be injured. It is relatively easy to be seriously injured,

PROTECT

and in real terms there are rarely any winners in genuine violent interactions.

It is also worth considering intent, which will inform your decision as to how much violence you might feel is appropriate. Bar brawls in UK high streets are broken up every night by the police or security staff and in many cases there are only relatively minor injuries. These might be described as a 'Grange Hill'; in other areas they are affectionately known as 'handbags'. Seeing this kind of activity on a regular basis can desensitise some people to violence. However, it is worth thinking about the reality of what is happening and how it differs from other violent crime. Apart from the fact that many young men who brawl may be too drunk to coordinate their actions, their intent is often to fight to establish a pecking order or for kudos. Most of the time their interactions are limited to trading punches and a bit of drunken grappling on the floor. Their aim, and therefore the level of violence they are prepared to inflict, is on a completely different level from that of someone whose intent is to kill or to find sexual gratification. The young man picking a fight with you on a Saturday night is not the same as the man lurking in the shadows with a sharpened screwdriver. Your interactions with the two will be completely

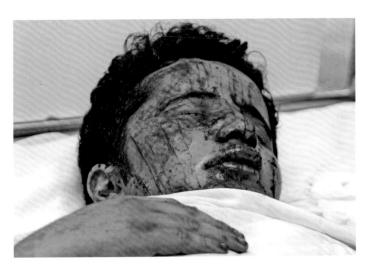

Be under no illusion. If you enter into a violent interaction, there is every chance you will be injured.

different. You should match your intent and therefore your actions with that of your attacker, but be prepared to escalate the situation if you need to do so to stay safe.

Finally, you must consider the hard truths of violence. TV representations bear almost no resemblance to the harsh reality of a collapsed airway following a strike to the throat, the trauma around an eye socket after the eye has been forced out, or the horror of facial trauma after someone has been repeatedly kicked in the face. Violence should always be the very last option.

Most of us hate the idea of having to use violence and would do so only if we absolutely felt we needed to protect ourselves. If you ever have the misfortune to be in this position, you will be less concerned about how cool it looks and much more concerned about protecting yourself and delivering effective violence to the person who has caused the problem.

In order to keep things as simple as possible we will look at three basic areas:

- *protecting yourself from strikes*

- *delivering effective violence*

- *getting out of holds*

Protecting yourself from strikes

There are many ways of blocking an attacker; we will use the most simple. For a punch or strike above the waist, use your forearm in an instinctive manner. If someone is trying to punch you, you will naturally move your head in the opposite direction; support this movement by throwing your forearm at the punching arm. Try to use the bony bit of your arm that runs from the point of your elbow to the outside edge of your wrist. Practise what this feels like; you will find that it helps to rotate your arm a bit as you push

PROTECT

it at a punch. We use this part of the arm for a number of reasons; first, because it is bony it will hurt the attacker more; secondly, it is less likely to be badly damaged (if you are being attacked with a knife, this area can be quite deeply cut and you can still maintain use of your hands); and, thirdly, if you aim to use this part of the arm, your physical stance will be about right to give you the best balance. The picture shows the forearm being used to block punches and strikes with a weapon. Note how the arm is pushed outwards, not to stop the punch, but to deflect the power away from you. This will put your attacker off balance, which is something you can use to your advantage.

If someone is trying to strike with a kick, then you may naturally respond by blocking with your legs. Try to avoid using your legs, as it inevitably means you are left standing on one leg and therefore vulnerable. Rather than kick out, lift your knee to present the shin rather than the thigh. Better still, keep both feet on the ground and simply bend to use your arms to gather up your opponent's leg.

Blocking with an arm.

Blocking with a leg or foot.

Do not worry too much about the technical issues of blocking. The key is to get something between your vulnerable areas and the strike being thrown, and rather than stop the energy to push it away from the body. The chances are you will not be able to block for ever, so the aim is to block the attacker off balance and strike very early in any attack.

PROTECT

Delivering effective violence

It is worth mentioning again that, while you have the absolute right to defend yourself using reasonable force, the law is quite rightly there to protect all of us. If you decide to attack someone in a premeditated way, inflict harm on someone who has ceased to pose a threat or deliberately carry or use a weapon, then you can expect to be on the wrong side of the law.

Defending yourself with reasonable force includes using items that you may have to hand – for example, an umbrella, keys or something in your home. However, you cannot carry something for the specific purpose of use as a weapon. The overall principle in law is that, once you have stunned an attacker and are able to make an escape, you should do so. If you have managed to overcome an attacker, you should not strike him or her again, and if you can make an escape without using violence, then you should do so.

If you reach the point where you need to deliver some form of violence to make an escape, then it is important to act as efficiently as possible.

Bearing all this in mind we should consider how and where we might strike.

Where to strike

There are three general areas to aim for:

Face and head. Aim for the soft bits – eyes, nose, throat. You can also easily damage ears and inflict pain by pulling hair. Finally the mouth is very sensitive, but keep your fingers away. It is also worthy of note that when most nerves in the neck are triggered there is an involuntary movement. So, if you twist an attacker's head, the entire body tends to go with it.

The chest is relatively well protected, so it is usually easier to attack the groin. Shins and feet are an easy target to hit.

Torso. The solar plexus is vulnerable but can also be easy to miss if you don't know what you're doing. The testicles and female genital area are also good locations to attack.

Legs. Used mostly to disable, strikes to the thigh can render the target unable to walk. More importantly, the shins and feet can easily be attacked with the sharp edges of a shoe.

How to strike

There are a number of ways of inflicting a strike:

Using your body. Without anything to hand you are limited to your natural weapons, which are your hands, elbows, feet/shins, knees, teeth and head. Each of your natural weapons can be used to target almost any part of the body, so there is little point in describing in detail every possibility; it is up to you to decide what might have the best effect. In general terms, though, it is worth considering:

PROTECT

- Instinctively, you may try to punch or use the open palm to strike. If you are going to do so, it is normally best to choose an area to attack that is relatively unprotected and easy to strike quickly – for example, the throat or nose.

- If you are too close to strike with your hands effectively, then you can still use your fingers - and specifically, if you have them, nails – to attack soft areas of the face or the groin.

- If you are really close and unable to use your hands, then a short sharp knee to the groin is tremendously effective.

- If you are really close and unable to strike, then do not be afraid to bite. A bite to the face is tremendously painful and may give you the short time you need to make an escape.

- Avoid flamboyant kicking, as it brings your feet off the ground and puts you off balance. If you are being held from behind, a quick stamp downwards with a high heel to the foot or down the attacker's shin is the most effective use of your feet as weapons.

Using something to hand. If you are on the streets then it is normal to expect that you will be carrying small items such as keys or a pen, and perhaps a longer item – for example, an umbrella. At home this general theme is repeated: you might be able to reach small items such as a fork or rolling pin and longer items such as a golf club or broom handle.

In almost all instances you are better off 'jabbing' upwards with an item you are protecting yourself with, rather than trying to use it in a downward 'stabbing' or baseball 'swinging' action. With a small item you probably have to aim for the face or throat to have an effect, but a longer item, such as an umbrella, is very effective to the chest or solar plexus.

Self-Defence

When holding a set of keys or a pen, first hold it in a clenched fist with the sharp end coming out by your thumb, then use your thumb to fix it in place. Remember it is the initial shock of your attack that will give you the time to escape, so once you have attacked there is no need to hang around. Strike and run.

When holding a longer item such as an umbrella or stick, use both hands and keep the item low and close to you. Again, remember you are looking to give yourself the opportunity to escape, so strike quickly and firmly to disable your attacker and then look to escape.

Remember, however you decide to attack, you can use only reasonable force. In any encounter, you will make decisions in the heat of the moment that may be scrutinised later in a court. In some extreme instances reasonable force includes incapacitating your attacker, but it is always best to err on the side of caution. If you can make an escape without using violence then do so. Violence should always be the last resort.

Getting out of holds

If you are held from behind in a head lock, move your fingers to the crook of the elbow and turning your head create space to breathe. Then move to strike.

If you are being held, it is because the attack is in a transitional phase – for example, you are being restrained prior to being sexually attacked or prior to being transferred to a car – or because your attacker is trying to cause damage – using a head lock to strangle or an arm lock. Here are some classic holds. You will see that all fit to the same pattern: ensure you can breathe, loosen the hold and then inflict violence.

PROTECT

Release yourself from a neck grab by forcing your arms rapidly up or down between your attacker's arms. Then move to strike and run.

If you are held from behind, you can attack the genitals with the hand, the shin with your heel or the face with the back of your head. Strike quickly and aggressively and prepare to run.

If you are among the majority of people who will never receive formal self-defence training, it is important to have some idea of what you might do if you ever found yourself having to use violence. The advice above will hopefully have given you something to think about, if nothing else. The best overall advice is to keep it simple and keep thinking. Try not to become emotionally involved; think of it as a task that you must complete to ensure your safety. Your aim should not be to fight someone to a standstill; you should use enough force to allow you to escape with your own safety. So, putting it all together, the stages you might expect to go though in an escalating situation are:

- ○ *Attempt to de-escalate by talking.*

- ○ *Keep talking and use calm but firm body language. Think! Look for the opportunity to disengage. Consider any weapons to hand.*

- ○ *Block the attack when it comes and try to put the attacker off balance.*

- ○ *Quickly move to strike with aggression and determination. Inflict a level of violence sufficient to allow you to escape.*

- ○ *Disengage rapidly (run away).*

Of course, at the other end of the spectrum you may find yourself having to decide to strike someone first because they are coming up your stairs in the middle of the night. Whatever you do, keep thinking, and, if you do decide to act physically, don't mess about.

PROTECT

Websites and Sources of Further Information

You may find the following websites of interest if you would like further information relating to your own personal security. All were checked in December 2006.

www.bbc.co.uk The BBC website. This has a wealth of information relating to both crime and terrorism. It is presented in an excellent format and is easy to read and digest. More importantly, the BBC runs a system called 'connecting in a crisis'. This is its requirement, as a public-service broadcaster, to adjust its programming in the event of an emergency and to carry public information. If you follow the links to **www.bbc.co.uk/radio** you will be able to find the frequency for your local radio station or listen to it online.

www.bsi-global.com The home page for the British Standards Institute. It gives information about the relevant standards for security and fire-related equipment. You can also order guidebooks concerning the physical security of your business.

www.bsia.co.uk The website for the British Security Industry Association, one of the regulatory bodies. It includes security advice and information on local approved companies.

www.bullying.co.uk The UK's website providing guidance for children, parents and professionals on dealing with bullying.

www.crimereduction.gov.uk A website aimed at those in the crime reduction community. It contains articles on criminology and crime initiatives. If you want to learn more about crime as an academic subject, this is a useful site.

www.crimestatistics.org.uk Details of the police-recorded crime in your area and also the British Crime Survey.

www.expeditionmedicine.co.uk The leading provider of expedition and wilderness medical training courses.

www.fco.gov.uk The home page for the Foreign & Commonwealth Office, which looks after UK interests worldwide. This website contains probably the most comprehensive travel advice section anywhere on the Web and is kept absolutely up to date. You may find that your travel insurance company will not cover you if you go against the advice of the FCO website. (You can also follow a link from this site to the MI6 website **www.sis.gov.uk**.)

www.firekills.gov.uk The government's website offering advice on fire prevention. You can download an excellent home guide dealing with fire prevention from this site. You can also find details of your local fire prevention officer and advice about smoke detectors and other fire equipment.

www.gogapyear.com UK advice for students embarking on a gap-year holiday.

www.homeoffice.gov.uk The Home Office website is an excellent start point if you are looking for information about crime or terrorism in the UK. There are specific sections giving up-to-date advice on how to prevent crime or terrorism and of course the current threat state of the UK. You can also find information about drugs, anti-social behaviour and a whole lot more – a very useful government site indeed.

www.iam.org.uk The website for the Institute of Advanced Motorists. This UK charity champions road safety and provides driver training approved by both police and insurance companies.

www.identity-theft.org.uk The UK Government's website providing advice and assistance relating to the theft of your identity.

www.locksmiths.co.uk The website for the Master Locksmiths Association (MLA). You can search for a registered locksmith in your area and read guidelines for the minimum recommended security for your home.

www.mi5.gov.uk The main Security Service website. It provides advice on the most up-to-date threats and also offers security guidance to businesses through the National Security Advice Centre. The site has links to other websites dealing with security-related matters in the UK.

www.nhs.uk The home page for the NHS. This site has everything you could possibly need about your family's health. Of particular interest, the NHS Direct pages have the most up-to-date travel medical advice, and there is a good section on first aid.

www.niscc.gov.uk The website for the National Infrastructure Security Coordination Centre. This protects the UK national infrastructure from electronic attack; if your business operates a network, it can offer useful advice.

nsi.org.uk The home page of the National Security Inspectorate, which tests and inspects companies that provide security and fire equipment.

www.patient.co.uk A website run in conjunction with UK GPs. If you type PTSD into its search engine, it will give you links to all the current post-traumatic stress disorder assistance available. It also has a very handy self-help guide that is worth reading if you think you may be suffering from trauma-induced stress. The main organisations it will link you to include:

DISASTER ACTION: **www.disasteraction.org.uk** 01483 799066

DISASTER AFTER CARE SERVICES: 01249 824859

THE TRAUMA CENTRE: **www.trauma999.co.uk** 01792 512063

TRAUMA STRESS CLINIC: 0207 530 3666

www.police.uk The UK national site for police forces. You will find a link to the website for your local police force. Each police force has details on its website of how to get in touch with its community crime prevention officers and counterterrorist security advisers. Most police force websites also have up-to-date information about security measures for your home, including approved locksmiths and alarm companies.

www.preparingforemergencies.gov.uk The government's primary source of information to the general public about what to do in the event of an emergency. It is an excellent website and has huge amounts of advice.

www.redcross.org.uk/firstaid The website for the British Red Cross. This site contains basic first-aid advice and also gives details of first-aid courses you could attend. The National Helpline number is 0870 170922.

www.rospa.org The website for the Royal Society for the Prevention of Accidents. RoSPA works in all areas, including home, occupational, road, water and leisure safety. It runs a driver-training programme that is also recognised by the police and insurance companies. The site also holds some interesting statistics about how people end up injuring themselves every year.

www.soldsecure.com A non-profit organisation supported by the Home Office and the Master Locksmiths Association. It carries out trials on security equipment. You can find details of approved equipment on this site.

www.ssaib.org An organisation that provides certification for the providers of electronic burglar and fire alarm systems. You can find details of certified products and dealers on this site.

www.statistics.gov.uk The UK's main statistics site, where you can look up whether you are more likely to be seen by your doctor on time or involved in a car crash.

www.talktofrank.com Accurate and easily accessible advice for all ages relating to illegal drug use. Hotline: 0800 776600.

www.tfl.gov.uk The Transport for London home page. This gives details on all public transport in the capital. In the event of an emergency it posts bulletins outlining the best way to travel.

www.thatcham.org An organisation that provides a unique range of products and services to the insurance and motor repair industries and is best known for testing vehicle security systems.

www.the-kennel-club.org.uk The website for the Kennel Club. If you are considering buying a dog to keep you company and perhaps to act as a guard dog, there are a number of considerations. The leaflets 'Thinking of Buying a Dog' and 'Choosing the Right Dog for You' are both available online, as is advice on breeds.

www.travel.state.gov The US Department of State website giving advice to US citizens travelling abroad. This can be a useful cross-check for the FCO website and sometimes has information not contained on the FCO site.

www.traveline.org.uk A UK-wide service provided by local authorities and public-transport companies that assists in planning journeys. During a major incident it also posts information about alternative routes.

www.ukresilience.info The UK Government's civil contingency planning home page. It is aimed mostly at those who will be involved in the response to a major incident, but, if you want to understand a bit more about the plans in place, you can read the detail and legislation here.

PICTURE CREDITS

Empics: pp. 120, 152, 156
Jonathan Falconer: p. 105
Getty Images: pp. 19, 23, 26, 35–6, 44, 46, 48, 59, 64–6, 69–72, 75–6, 85, 88, 98, 101, 103, 106–7, 109, 111, 113, 115, 116–18, 122–3, 125–7, 129, 131–3, 135, 144–5, 147–9, 152, 159, 161–3, 168, 170–2, 177, 184, 191–3, 196, 200–1, 204, 209, 211–12, 214–15, 217, 223, 225, 227
Steve Gorton and Frances Leader: pp. 53–7
Lynwen Griffiths: pp. 13–21, 22, 24, 27, 30, 32, 47, 73, 76–8, 80–4, 86–93, 95–7, 99–100, 112, 137–40, 165, 173, 175–6, 178–80, 185–7, 189, 199, 219–20, 222, 229, 230–5
HM Government: p. 136
Chris Holt: pp. 24, 166
Tom Walford: p. 63

Index

242

Index

246